DECORATING WITH SLIPCOVERS

Refresh your furnishings with stylish, affordable slipcovers

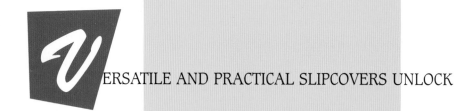ERSATILE AND PRACTICAL SLIPCOVERS UNLOCK

THE DECORATING POTENTIAL OF YOUR HOME. NO LONGER ARE YOU

COMMITTED TO A COLOR SCHEME OR DESIGN STYLE DICTATED BY YOUR FURNITURE.

NOR DO YOU HAVE TO BUY NEW FURNITURE TO GIVE YOUR HOME A NEW LOOK.

WITH THE ENDLESS SELECTION OF DECORATOR FABRICS AVAILABLE, YOU CAN

DESIGN AND SEW BEAUTIFUL SLIPCOVERS TO UPDATE YOUR DECOR

WITH RICH COLORS, PRINTS, AND TEXTURES THAT

EXPRESS YOUR PERSONAL TASTE.

SLIPCOVERS

SLIPCOVERS

Created by: The Editors of Cowles Creative Publishing, Inc.

Library of Congress Cataloging-in-Publication Data
Slipcovers.
        p.   cm. -- (Creative textiles)
    Includes index.
    ISBN 0-86573-411-9 (softcover)
    1. Slip covers.   I. Cowles Creative Publishing.   II. Series.
TT395.S534 1997
646.2'1--dc21   97-14622

THE HOME DECORATING INSTITUTE®

CONTENTS

EXPRESSIONS OF STYLE

Slipcovers offer you the opportunity to establish a new style and make a fresh decorating statement with your existing furniture. Though limited somewhat by your furniture's original design lines (a wing chair will always be a wing chair), you are free to make choices in the design of the slipcover that may change your furniture's character. For instance, a stately Edwardian wing chair, upholstered in elegant jacquard, is a mainstay in a formal, traditional living room. However, given a floral chintz slipcover with a ruffled skirt, it acquires a cheerful, romantic style, suitable for an English country bedroom. In the same manner, semifitted slipcovers make a formal sofa and chairs more appropriate for a relaxed lifestyle. And common metal folding chairs are unrecognizable under perky, room-brightening slipcovers.

A style change may not be what you want. The upholstery fabric on a favorite chair may be getting a little dingy or perhaps it simply no longer suits your color scheme. If the chair's padding is still firm and its frame is still sturdy, a fitted slipcover is a great

Notice the totally different looks that are achieved by changing the slipcover on this chair. The formal elegance of the leafy brocade slipcover (top left) makes it suitable for a traditional setting. Dressed in a large floral print with a gathered skirt, the chair adds romantic feminine charm to a living room or bedroom. The more

alternative to reupholstery. Hugging the lines of the chair as a glove fits a hand, a fitted slipcover gives the chair new life without losing its identity, and with far less commitment than stripping the original cover and reupholstering. Family heirlooms and cherished antiques retain their valuable "first skins" while playing an active role in your decorating plan.

Design features such as skirts, closures, welting, and other embellishments define the style of the slipcover and give you a palette for expressing your personality. A contemporary spirit may prefer the sleek lines and functional detailing of a semi-fitted slipcover with grommeted ties. Floral slipcovers with ruffled skirts and bows exude feminine country charm with a romantic twist. The nature lover is comfortable with the down-home country look of tab closures and cotton brush fringe on textured cotton slipcovers. Form-fitting slipcovers in elegant fabrics, accented with ornate gimp, cord, and tassels, divulge an appreciation for gracious living and traditional tastes.

tailored look of the plaid slipcover (top right), with its flat front arm panels and box-pleated skirt, makes it suitable for a masculine country den or family room. In a slipcover with geometric shapes and a metallic gleam (bottom right), the same chair has a more contemporary flavor.

COLORFUL INFLUENCES

Neutral color schemes are relaxing to the eye. Lots of pattern and texture, with variation in color values, keep the scheme interesting.

Color carries more clout in a decorating scheme than any other design element. Used effectively, color instills mood, influences size and temperature perceptions, and establishes harmony. Picture yourself in a vibrantly warm room, full of energy and cozy ambience. Most likely your vision includes shades of red, yellow, and orange. Add a fresh green plant here and there, and notice the slightly calming effect. Next, move into a cool, spacious room where the aura is serene and still. Are you seeing blues and greens? Add a touch of sunny yellow if you are feeling cold. Understanding the influences of colors, as well as the ways colors affect each other, can help you make wise color choices for slipcovers and cushions.

If you are working within a preexisting color scheme, it is important to understand the dynamics of that scheme to realize your options. If the color scheme is monochromatic, perhaps all blue, there must be variation in the values from light blue to dark blue in order to build interest into the scheme. A splash of warm color, perhaps with a yellow cushion or seat cover, enlivens the blues without breaking up the color scheme. However, the addition of a persimmon sofa slipcover, because of its size, changes the color scheme to complementary, and you will need to add other orange and gold accents to support the new color scheme.

An analogous color scheme successfully combines three to five closely related colors, and may include one primary color. For instance, various blue, purple, and violet hues harmonize well, as does a combination of various yellows and greens. Consider the size of the slipcover in relation to other elements in the room, and balance the colors in the scheme. By using a print fabric that combines all the colors in the scheme, the slipcover brings the other elements into harmony.

Working within a versatile neutral color scheme is perhaps easiest of all. Just remember to spice up the scheme with lots of texture and pattern variations and balance the light, medium, and dark color values throughout. If making a light slipcover for a sofa or large chair, consider using welting in a medium value to visually divide it into smaller sections. Partial covers and chair cushions offer opportunities for adding small splashes of dramatic color to a neutral room.

Complementrary color schemes keep the eye moving. Colors in the floral print fabric and wallpaper border are repeated individually in other room elements.

DESIGN ELEMENTS
Weaves, Prints & Textures

The vast range of decorator fabrics can be mind-boggling, but you can make the selection process easier by dividing the fabrics into categories and establishing a few guidelines. Determine the effect you want to create with your new slipcover or cushion, keeping in mind its size in relation to other elements in the room. While color and design play an important part in the decision, it is also important to consider the fiber content, weave structure, and any surface treatment applied to the fabric.

Decorator fabrics suitable for slipcovers are usually made of natural fibers, most often cotton, but also include linen, silk, and even wool. Natural fibers are breathable, comfortable, and easy to sew. Often they are treated with a stain-resistant or crease-resistant finish. Fabrics can be grouped into categories according to their weave or surface design. Plain weaves (a) are the simplest of weaves. They may be solid in color or printed, and their strength is determined by the closeness of the yarns in the weave. Satin weaves (b) are woven so that yarns float on the surface, giving the fabric a subtle sheen. They also may be solid in color or printed. If sheen is desired, a satin weave is a better choice than chintz (c), which gets its shine from a surface coating. It is difficult to remove creases from chintz, and the surface coating will wear off with use.

b

c

a

Jacquard weaves (d), including damasks, tapestries, and brocades, have woven-in designs. Novelty weaves (e), often solid colors, feature textural interest created by complicated weave patterns. These fabrics are very versatile in any color scheme.

Printed fabrics and jacquards are printed or woven to match from one selvage to the next, so that any necessary seams in large pieces are less visible. The *vertical repeat* is the vertical distance between points where the printed or woven pattern repeats itself. The *horizontal repeat* is often given, also, especially on larger prints. This is valuable information for determining the amount of fabric necessary for a slipcover. Large motifs in a pattern must be centered on cushion tops and bottoms, chair backs, and arms. Ideally, a pattern should flow uninterrupted from the top to the bottom of the slipcover.

The scale of a print is also an important consideration. Large prints may overpower a small chair slipcover, just as tiny all-over prints can get lost on a sofa slipcover. If you want to use several prints in the same room, select coordinating prints in various sizes, and add solid color accents.

d

e

TOTAL *C*OVERAGE

RELAXED & REFINED

ELEGANT & EXPRESSIVE

Fitted SLIPCOVERS

This close-fitting slipcover works equally well on a fully upholstered armchair or sofa. It can be made from a single fabric or several coordinating fabrics. For interest, add contrasting welting or brush fringe in the seams. The skirt may be made with tailored corner pleats or it may be made fully gathered or box-pleated.

A frequent concern about a slipcover is whether it will stay in place. To help secure the slipcover, an attached fabric strip, concealed under the skirt, is pinned to the existing fabric. Also, polyurethane foam pieces are tucked along the sides of the deck to provide a tight fit.

Sewing slipcovers is an alternative to upholstering. However, upholstering is required when the furniture needs structural repair, such as springing. It is easier to sew slipcovers for furniture that is fairly square, with straight lines, than it is for furniture with more details. Furniture with wood strips on the arm can be slipcovered if the arms are first wrapped with upholstery batting. Recliners should be upholstered because of the movable parts.

Furniture with a concave back design, such as a channel back or barrel back, is difficult to slipcover, and the slipcover may not fit well. For best results, a concave back should be wrapped or covered in a thick upholstery batting before it is slipcovered. Furniture with a tufted back or button back can be slipcovered, but the tufting and buttons are

eliminated in the slipcover. The back is wrapped with upholstery batting to fill it out for a smooth-fitting slipcover.

As a general rule, a chair requires about 7 to 8 yd. (6.4 to 7.35 m) of fabric; a love seat, 10 to 12 yd. (9.15 to 11.04 m); and a sofa, 16 to 20 yd. (14.72 to 18.4 m). These amounts include matching welting and a skirt with pleats at the corners. Allow additional fabric for cushions and ruffled or box-pleated skirts. Each cushion requires 1 to 1½ yd. (0.95 to 1.4 m) of fabric. For a ruffled or box-pleated skirt, allow 1 yd. (0.95 m) extra for a chair, 2 to 3 yd. (1.85 to 2.75 m) for a love seat, and 4 yd. (3.7 m) for a sofa.

LIST *of* MATERIALS

▶ Muslin for pin-fitting the pieces.
▶ Decorator fabric.
▶ Cording for welting; select soft, pliable cording with a cotton core.
▶ Zippers; one for chairs, two for sofas and love seats. The length of each zipper is 1" to 2" (2.5 to 5 cm) shorter than the length of the vertical seam at the side of the outside back. Additional zippers are needed for cushions (page 36).
▶ Upholstery batting, if necessary, to pad the existing furniture.
▶ Polyurethane foam, 2" (5 cm) strips, to insert at sides and back of deck.
▶ T-pins, tacks, or heavy-duty stapler and staples, for securing tacking strip to furniture.

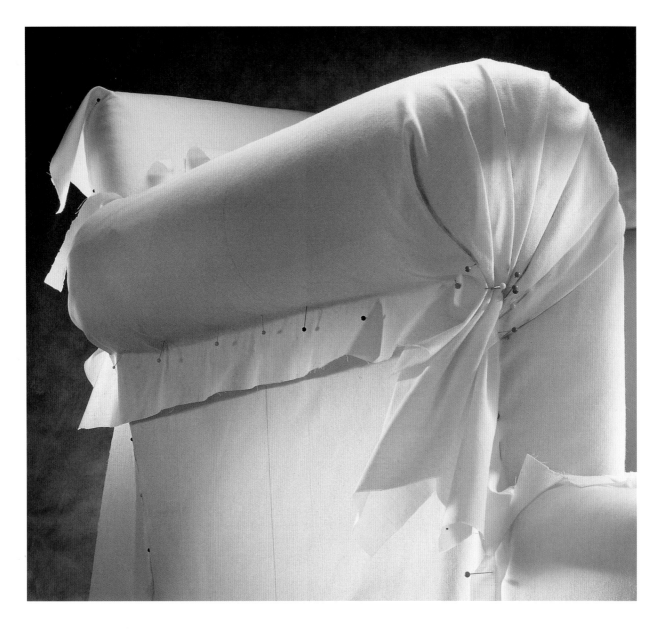

The easiest way to make a slipcover pattern is by pin-fitting muslin on the chair or sofa. Before you start, look carefully at the furniture. Usually the seams in the slipcover will be in the same locations as the seams on the existing cover, but you may be able to add or eliminate some details, provided it will not affect the fit of the slipcover. For example, if the existing cushions are wrap-style, you may want to slipcover them as box cushions with welting. Or a chair with a pleated front arm may be slipcovered with a separate front arm piece.

The style of the skirt can also be changed. You may want to gather a skirt all the way around the furniture, allowing double fullness. Or you may want bunched gathers at the corners of a chair, or at the corners and center front of a sofa. For a more tailored look, the skirt may have box pleats instead of gathers.

A chair with rolled arms and loose back and seat cushions is used in the instructions that follow. This example includes the details that are common to most furniture. Although your furniture style may be somewhat different, use these basic steps as a guide.

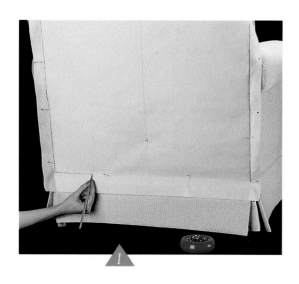

1 ...... Remove cushions. Measure outside back of chair or sofa between seamlines; cut muslin 3" to 4" (7.5 to 10 cm) larger than measurements. Mark centerline on outside back piece, following lengthwise grain. Pin to chair, smoothing fabric; mark seamlines.

2 ...... Measure inside back between seamlines; cut muslin 15" (38 cm) wider and about 10" (25.5 cm) longer than measurements. This allows for 6" (15 cm) at the lower edge to tuck into the deck and hold the slipcover in place. Mark centerline on inside back piece, following lengthwise grain.

3 ...... Pin outside back and inside back together along top of chair or sofa, matching centerlines. Fold out excess fabric on inside back piece at upper corner, forming a dart. Pin muslin snugly, but do not pull fabric tight.

4 ...... Trim excess fabric on sides of inside back to 2" (5 cm); clip along arms as necessary for smooth curve. Push about 1/2" (1.3 cm) of fabric into crevices on sides and lower edge of inside back; mark seamlines by pushing pencil into crevices.

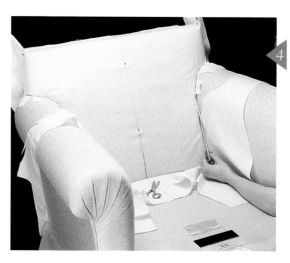

PATTERN FOR A PLEATED ARM

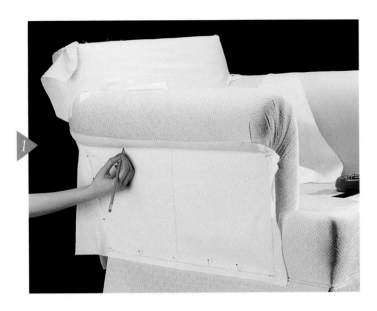

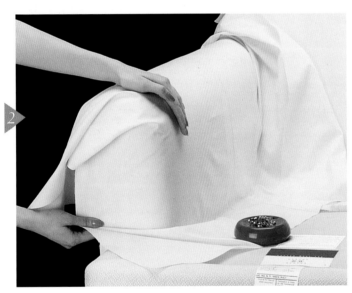

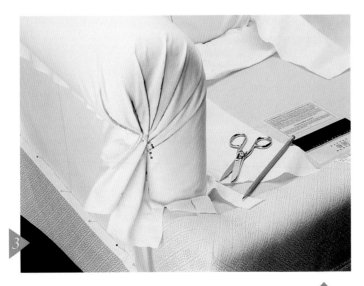

1...... Measure outside arm between seamlines; cut muslin 3" (7.5 cm) larger than measurements. Mark lengthwise grainline on muslin. Pin outside arm in place, with grainline perpendicular to floor and with lower edge extending 1/2" (1.3 cm) beyond seamline at upper edge of skirt. Smooth fabric upward; pin. Pin outside arm to outside back. Mark seamlines.

2...... Measure inside arm from deck to seamline at upper edge of outside arm, and from inside back to front of arm; cut muslin about 9" (23 cm) larger than measurements. Mark lengthwise grainline on muslin. Pin inside arm piece in place, with 7" (18 cm) extending at inside back and grainline straight across arm, smoothing fabric up and around arm.

3...... Pin inside arm to outside arm at front; clip and trim fabric at front lower edge as necessary for a smooth fit. Pleat out fabric for rolled arm to duplicate pleats in existing fabric. Mark radiating foldlines of pleats.

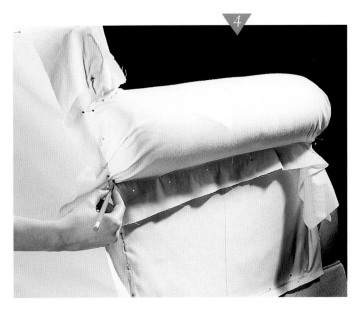

4 ...... Make tucks on inside arm at back of chair, to fold out excess fabric; clip inside arm as necessary for smooth fit. Mark seamline at beginning and end of tucks on inside arm and outside back.

5 ...... Mark inside arm and inside back with large dots, about halfway up the arm. Push about ½" (1.3 cm) of fabric on inside arm into crevices at deck and back.

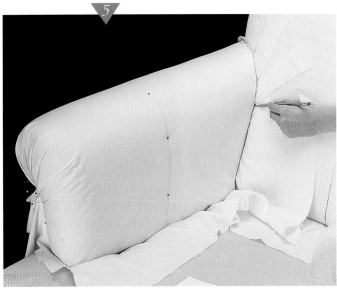

6 ...... Mark all seamlines on muslin, smoothing the fabric as you go.

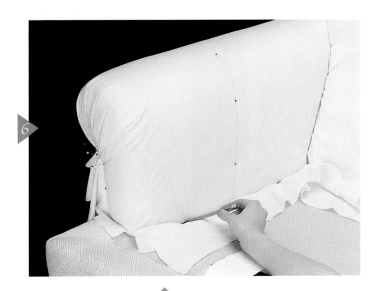

HOW TO PIN-FIT THE

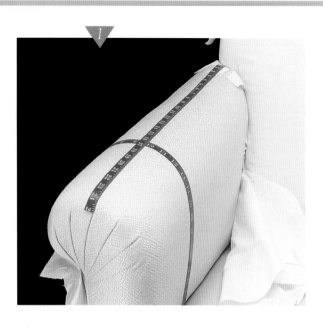

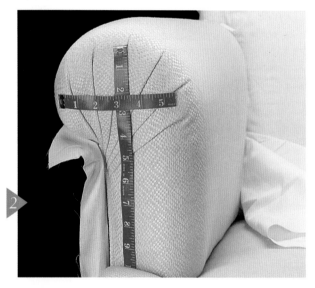

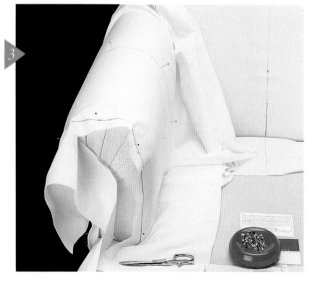

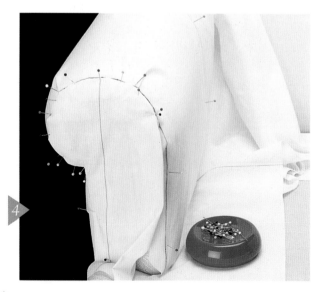

1...... Follow page 18, step 1, for outside arm. Measure inside arm from deck to seamline at upper edge of outside arm, and from inside back to front edge of arm; cut muslin about 9" (23 cm) larger than these measurements. Mark lengthwise grainline on muslin.

2...... Measure front of the arm; cut muslin 2" to 3" (5 to 7.5 cm) larger than measurements. Mark lengthwise grainline on muslin.

3...... Pin inside arm piece in place, with 7" (18 cm) extending at inside back and grainline straight across arm, smoothing fabric up and around arm. Mark seamline at front edge of arm; trim away excess fabric not needed for seam allowances.

4...... Pin front arm piece in place. Fold out excess fabric on inside arm as necessary to fit front arm piece, making two pleats. Mark seamline for curve of arm, following existing seamline on chair. Complete pattern as on page 19, steps 4, 5, and 6.

HOW TO PIN-FIT THE *P*ATTERN FOR THE DECK

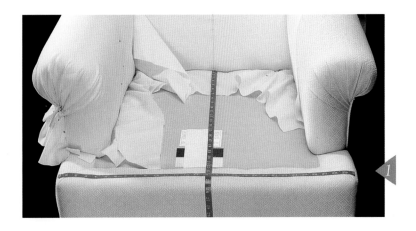

1...... Measure width at front of deck; measure length of deck, down front of chair to skirt seam; cut muslin 15" (38 cm) wider and 9" (23 cm) longer than the measurements. Mark centerline on muslin, following grainline. Mark seamline on muslin at front edge on straight of grain, 1/2" (1.3 cm) from raw edge.

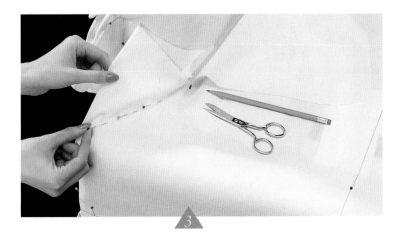

2...... Pin marked line on muslin to welting of skirt seam, with centerline centered on skirt; this positions muslin on straight of grain. Smooth muslin over front edge and deck, and match centerlines of deck and back.

3...... Mark deck and inside arm pieces with large dots, at point where deck meets front of inside arm. For furniture with T-cushion, clip excess deck fabric to dot. Fold out excess fabric on deck at front corner, forming a dart; pin and mark.

4...... Pin deck to outside arm piece at side of chair; mark seamline. Do not fit deck snug. Push about 1/2" (1.3 cm) of fabric into crevices at sides and back of deck; mark seamlines by pushing pencil into crevices.

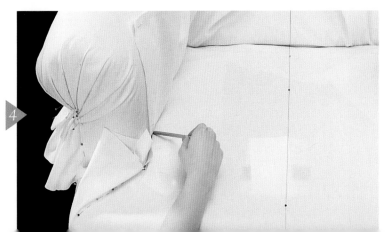

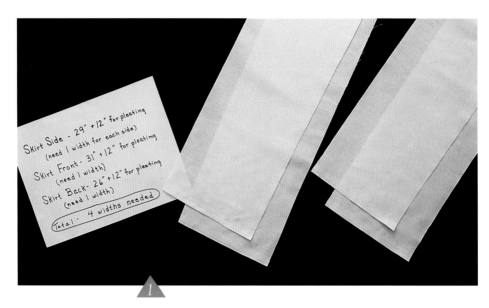

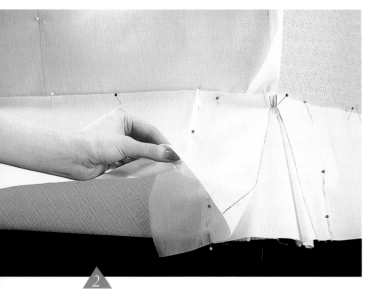

1...... Measure for skirt around sides, front, and back to determine cut width of skirt; allow for gathers or pleats. Plan seam placement, based on width of fabric and size of furniture, so seams are concealed in gathers or pleats whenever possible; plan a seam at back corner where zipper will be inserted. Cut number of fabric widths needed; cut muslin pieces 1" (2.5 cm) longer than length of skirt.

2...... Place raw edge of muslin just below lower edge of skirt; pin at upper edge of skirt, keeping muslin straight and even. Pin seams as you come to them; pin out fullness for pleats or gathers. Pin vertical tucks in skirt, pinning 1/8" (3 mm) tuck near back corner on each side of chair and 1/4" (6 mm) tuck near each corner on back of chair; tucks will be released in step 3, opposite, adding ease to skirt. Mark seams and placement of pleats or gathers.

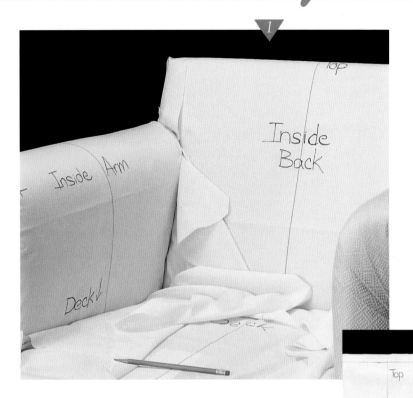

1...... Mark upper edge of all muslin pieces; label pieces. Check that all seamlines, darts, gathers, and pleats are marked. Mark dots at intersecting seams; label.

2...... Remove muslin. Add ¼" (6 mm) ease to back edge of outside arm at lower corner. Add ½" (1.3 cm) ease to sides of outside back at lower corners. Taper to marked seamlines at upper corners.

3...... Remove the pinned tucks near back corners of skirt pieces. Mark "foldline" at lower edge of muslin for self-lined skirt.

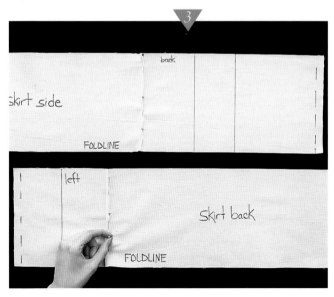

continued

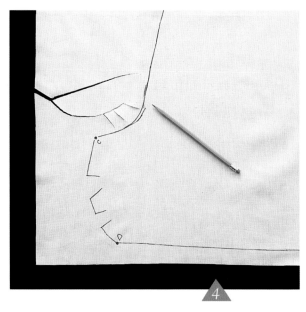

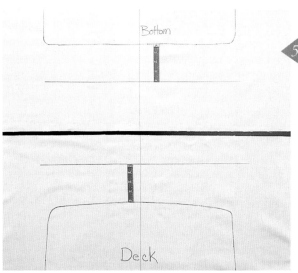

4 ..... True straight seamlines, using straightedge; true curved seam-lines, drawing smooth curves. Do not mark seamlines in pleated areas.

5 ..... Add 4" (10 cm) to lower edge of inside back and back edge of deck.

6 ..... Mark the lower edge of inside arm from a point 4" (10 cm) away from seamline at back edge to ½" (1.3 cm) from large dot at front edge; repeat for sides of deck.

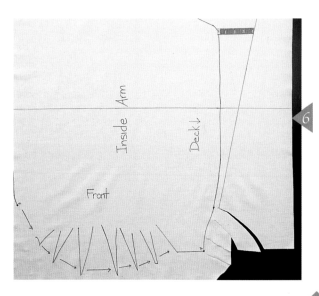

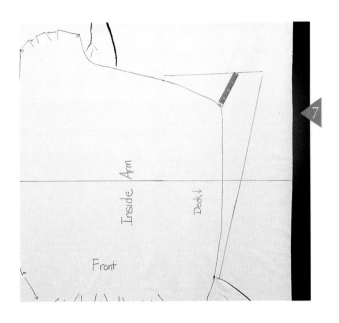

7 ..... Mark back edge of inside arm from a point 4" (10 cm) away from seamline at the lower edge to ½" (1.3 cm) from large dot; repeat for sides of inside back.

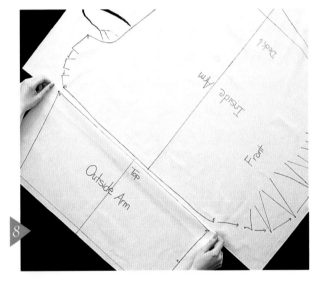

8 ..... Check lengths of seamlines for adjoining seams; adjust as necessary to ensure that seamlines match.

9 ..... Fold pleats on marked lines. Mark seamlines in pleated area; add ½" (1.3 cm) seam allowances. Trim on cutting line through all layers of pleats. Add ½" (1.3 cm) seam allowances to any remaining seams. Cut pieces on marked lines.

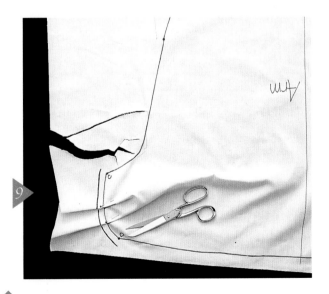

Laying out & Cutting
THE FABRIC

Whenever possible, lay out all the pattern pieces on the fabric before you start to cut. This allows you to rearrange the pieces as necessary to make the best use of the fabric. For boxed cushions, follow the cutting directions on page 37.

When a patterned fabric with an all-over design is used for slipcovers, little matching is required. When seaming widths of fabric together, such as for a sofa, the pattern may be matched as on page 28. Patterned fabrics may also be matched at the seamline on the upper edge of the skirt, if desired, following the technique for boxed cushions (page 41). If a patterned fabric with a one-way design is used, be careful to lay the pieces in the correct direction on the fabric.

Center large motifs in a print fabric on the top and the bottom of the cushion. For best results, also align the design so it continues down the back of the furniture, onto the cushion, and down the skirt.

In addition to the pieces cut from the muslin pattern, you will need a 3" (7.5 cm) tacking strip cut on the straight of grain. This strip is used to secure the slipcover to the furniture with T-pins, tacks, or staples. Cut the length of the tacking strip equal to the distance around the furniture at the upper edge of the skirt.

Cut fabric strips for the welting as on page 42. Measure the seamlines that will have welting to determine the total length of the bias strips you will need to cut.

TIPS FOR LAYING OUT & CUTTING
THE SLIPCOVER FABRIC

Center large motifs, such as floral clusters, on the back, sides, cushions, and on the top of the arms.

Center the prominent stripe of a striped fabric on the center placement line of the outside and inside back pieces and on the cushion pieces. Decide in which direction the stripes will run on the arms; usually it is preferable to have the stripes run in the same direction as the stripes on the skirt.

Cut the skirt pieces for a self-lined skirt, placing the foldline at lower edge of skirt on a crosswise fold of the fabric. Self-lined skirts hang better than single-layer skirts with a hem.

Cut arm pieces, right sides together, using the first piece as the pattern for cutting the second piece.

continued

TIPS FOR LAYING OUT & CUTTING
THE SLIPCOVER FABRIC (CONTINUED)

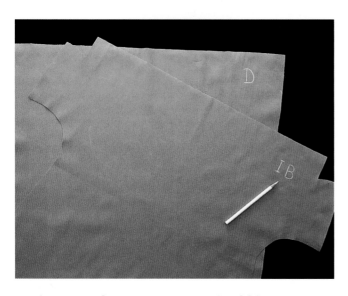

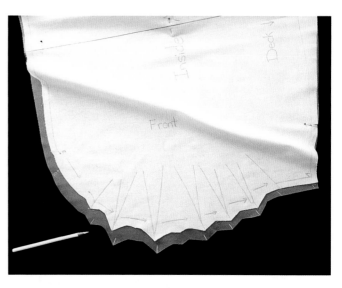

Mark names of pieces on wrong side of fabric, using chalk. Abbreviations like "D" for deck, "IB" for inside back, and "OA" for outside arm may be used.

Transfer all markings, including notches and dots, from the muslin pieces to the slipcover fabric.

HOW TO MATCH A PATTERNED FABRIC

1 ..... Position fabric widths, right sides together, matching selvages. Fold back the upper selvage until pattern matches; lightly press foldline.

2 ..... Unfold selvage; pin fabric widths together on foldline. Check match from right side.

3 ..... Repin the fabric widths so pins are perpendicular to the foldline; stitch on the foldline, using a straight stitch. Trim fabric to finished length.

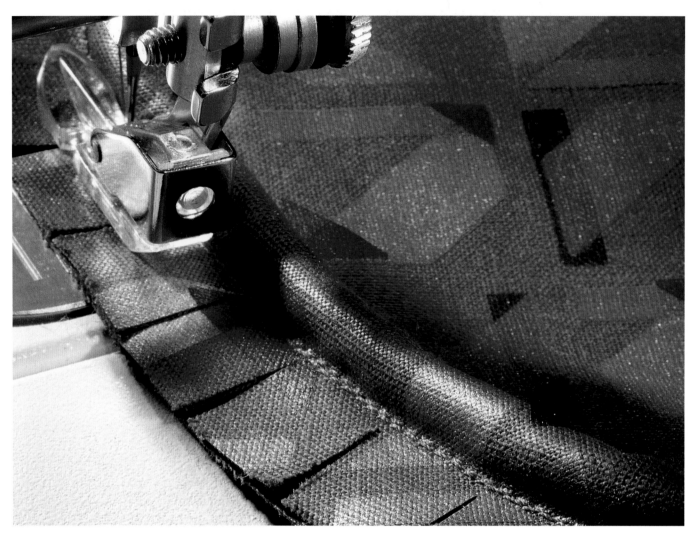

SEWING THE *Fitted* SLIPCOVER

Although the slipcover for your piece of furniture may be somewhat different from the style shown, many of the construction steps will be the same. It will be helpful for you to lay out the pieces and think through the sequence for sewing the seams of your slipcover. The labeled notches on adjoining seams will help you see how the pieces are to be joined together. To minimize the handling of bulky quantities of fabric, stitch any small details, such as darts, before assembling the large pieces.

For durable seams, use a strong thread, such as long-staple polyester, and a medium stitch length of about 10 stitches per inch (2.5 cm). Because slipcovers have several thicknesses of fabric at intersecting seams with welting, use a size 90/14 or 100/16 sewing machine needle.

Add welting to any seams that will be subjected to stress and wear, because welted seams are stronger than plain seams. For decorative detailing, welting can also be added to seams such as around the outside back and at the upper edge of the skirt. On furniture with front arm pieces, welting is usually applied around the front arm as a design detail. To prevent welted seams from puckering, take care not to stretch either the welting or the fabric as the seam is stitched. When a welted seam will be intersected by another seam, remove ½" (1.3 cm) of cording from the end of the welting to prevent bulk at the seamline.

For a chair, apply a zipper to one of the back seams of the slipcover. For a sofa, apply zippers to both back seams.

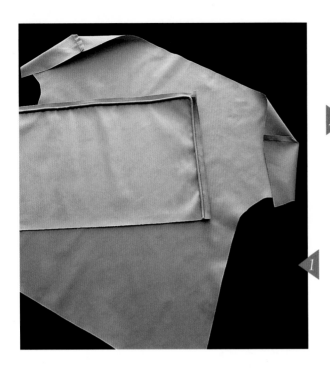

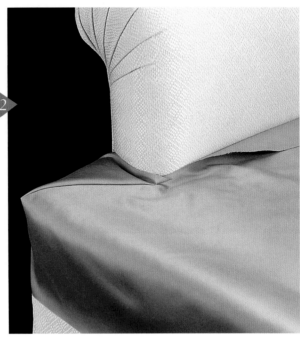

1 ...... Stitch darts at upper corners of inside back. If welting is desired, apply it to upper and front edges of outside arm, pivoting at corner.

2 ...... Stitch darts at outer front corners of deck; stop stitching ½" (1.3 cm) from raw edge at inner corner.

3 ...... Stitch deck to front of arm and inside arm; this can be stitched as two separate seams.

4 ...... Pin pleats in place at front and back of arm. Check the fit over arm of chair. Baste in place on seamline.

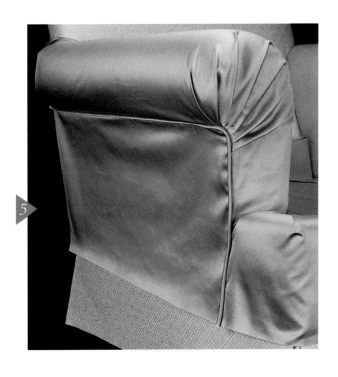

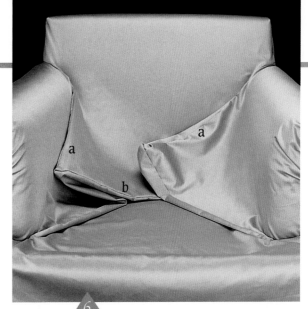

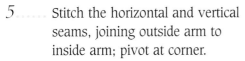

5   Stitch the horizontal and vertical seams, joining outside arm to inside arm; pivot at corner.

6   Pin inside arms to inside back on both sides (a). Pin lower edge of inside back to back edge of deck (b). Make tucks in seams at corners, if necessary, so pieces fit together. Stitch seams.

7   Apply welting around sides and upper edge of slipcover unit (page 43); curve ends of welting into seam allowance ½" (1.3 cm) from the lower edges (arrow). Join slipcover unit to outside back, leaving seam open for zipper application. Apply welting to lower edge.

8   Stitch skirt pieces together, leaving seam at back corner unstitched for zipper insertion; press seams open. Fold skirt in half lengthwise, wrong sides together; press.

continued

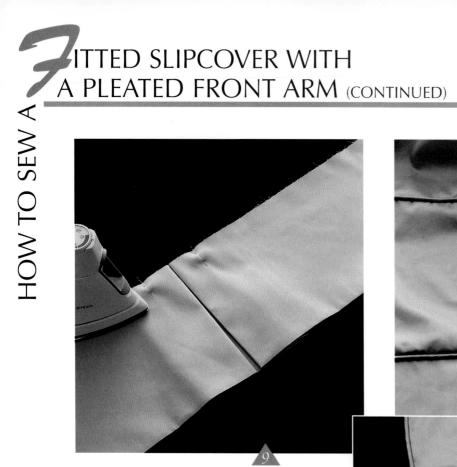

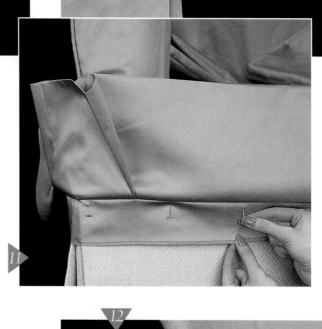

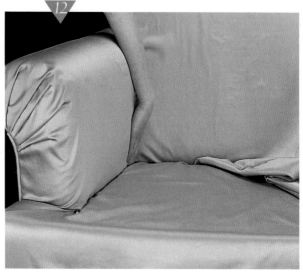

9...... Press pleats for pleated skirt. Or for gathered skirt, stitch gathering stitches by zigzagging over a cord as on page 110, step 6; for skirt with bunched gathers, stitch gathering stitches between the markings.

10.... Pin tacking strip to upper edge of skirt on wrong side. Join the skirt to adjoining pieces; for gathered skirt, pull up gathers to fit. Apply zipper (pages 34 and 35). Sew cushions (pages 38 to 41).

11.... Apply slipcover to furniture. Secure tacking strip to furniture by pinning into upholstery with T-pins.

12.... Push extra fabric allowance into crevices around the deck and inside back. Stuff 2" (5 cm) strips of polyurethane foam into crevices around deck to keep fabric from pulling out. Insert cushions.

HOW TO SEW A FITTED SLIPCOVER
WITH FRONT ARM PIECE

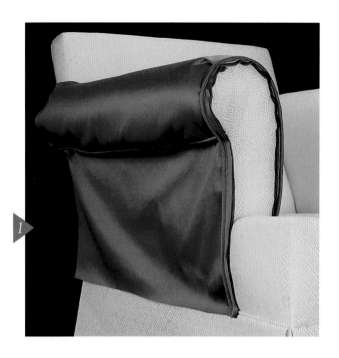

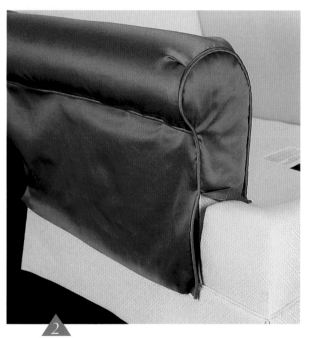

1...... Stitch darts at upper corners of inside back. Apply welting to the upper edge of inside arm, if desired. Stitch horizontal seam, joining the outside arm to the inside arm. Pin and baste tucks at front edge of inside/outside arm. Apply welting to front edge of inside/outside arm.

2...... Stitch the front arm piece to the front edge of inside/outside arm; stop stitching 2" (5 cm) from outer end of front arm piece.

3...... Follow steps 2 and 3 on page 30. Pin pleats in place at back of arm; baste in place on seamline.

4...... Complete vertical seam at front edge of outside arm. Finish the slipcover as in steps 6 to 12 on pages 31 and 32.

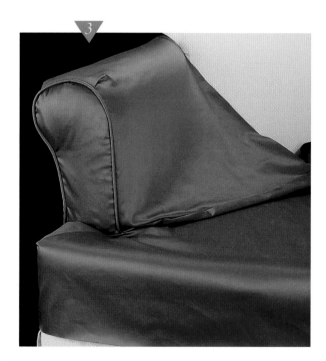

HOW TO APPLY THE

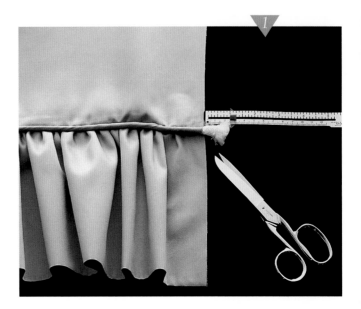

1...... Pull the cording out slightly from ends of skirt opening; trim off ends 1" (2.5 cm). Pull seam to return cording to original position.

2...... Press under seam allowances on zipper opening. Place open zipper on welted side of seam, so welting just covers zipper teeth and with zipper tab at lower edge. Pin in place; fold in seam allowance at lower edge of skirt to miter. Fold up end of zipper tape.

3...... Edgestitch on skirt, using zipper foot, with zipper teeth positioned close to folded edge. Stitch in the ditch of the welted seam.

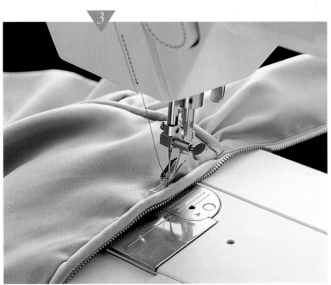

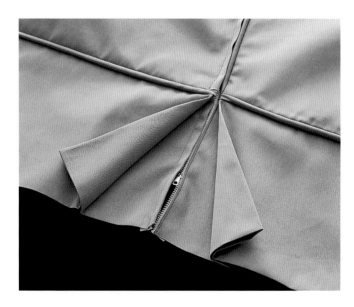

4 ..... Close zipper. Place remaining side of zipper under seam allowance, with folded edge at welted seamline. Pin in place; fold in seam allowance at lower edge of skirt to miter. Fold up end of zipper tape.

5 ..... Open zipper. Stitch 3/8" (1 cm) from folded edge, pivoting at top of zipper.

Pleated skirt. Follow steps 1 to 5, opposite, except break stitching at upper edge of the skirt. On skirt, stitch through lower layer of box pleat; stitch as close as possible to seam at upper edge of skirt.

Slipcovers
FOR BOXED CUSHIONS

You can make slipcovers for cushions on benches or window seats, as well as on sofas or chairs. Often cushions have welting at the edges, which adds strength to the seams. Plain welting (page 42) is most commonly used, but brush fringe or twisted welting may also be used. Slipcovers for cushions are made to fit snug on most slipcovers. However, for a more casual look, you can make a semifitted cushion slipcover.

To make it easier to insert the cushion, install a zipper across the back of the slipcover, extending around about 4" (10 cm) on each side. For cushions that are exposed on three sides, install a zipper across the back of the slipcover only. Use upholstery zippers, which are available in longer lengths than dressmaker zippers. The tab of the zipper will be concealed in a pocket at the end of the zipper opening. This is an upholsterer's technique that gives a professional finish.

CUTTING DIRECTIONS

For a fitted boxed cushion slipcover, cut the top and bottom pieces 1" (2.5 cm) larger than the cushion size to allow for seam allowances. For a semifitted slipcover, cut the top and bottom pieces 1½" (3.8 cm) larger than the cushion size, allowing for ½" (1.3 cm) seam allowance and ¼" (6 mm) ease on all sides. T-cushions are pin-fitted, using muslin, to ensure accurate cutting. Cut a boxing strip the length of the cushion front plus twice the length of the cushion side; the width of the boxing strip for a fitted slipcover is equal to the thickness of the cushion plus 1" (2.5 cm) for seam allowances. For a semi-fitted slipcover, the cut width of the boxing strip is equal to the thickness of the cushion plus 1¼" (3.2 cm) for two ½" (1.3 cm) seam allowances and ¼" (6 mm) ease. Seam strips together, as necessary. Cut two zipper strips, each the length of the zipper tape; the width of each zipper strip on a fitted slipcover is equal to one-half the thickness of the cushion plus 1" (2.5 cm) for seam allowances. For a semifitted slipcover, the width of each zipper strip is equal to one-half the thickness of the cushion plus 1⅛" (2.8 cm) for seam allowances and ease. Cut welting strips for plain welting (page 42).

LIST *of* MATERIALS

▸ Decorator fabric.
▸ Zipper, about 8" (20.5 cm) longer than back edge of cushion.
▸ Fabric and cording for fabric-covered welting; or brush fringe or twisted welting.

HOW TO CUT THE FABRIC FOR A T-CUSHION

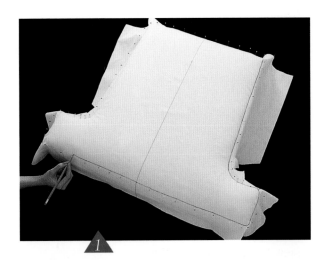

1 ...... *Fitted T-cushion.* Cut muslin about 4" (10 cm) larger than top of cushion; mark grainline at center of fabric. Place muslin over cushion; pin along seamlines, smoothing out fabric. Mark seamlines along pin marks.

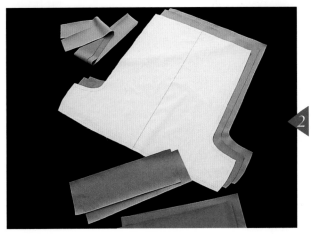

2 ...... Remove muslin. True seamlines, using straightedge. Fold muslin in half to check that piece is symmetrical; make any necessary adjustments. Add ½" (1.3 cm) seam allowances. Cut cushion top and bottom from slipcover fabric. Cut zipper and boxing strips, above. Mark wrong side of fabric pieces, using chalk.

Semifitted T-cushion. Follow steps 1 and 2 above for a T-cushion; in step 2, add ½" (1.3 cm) seam allowances and ¼" (6 mm) ease to all sides.

1 ...... Press under ½" (1.3 cm) seam allowance on one long edge of each zipper strip. Position folded edges of strips along center of zipper teeth, right sides up. Using zipper foot, topstitch ⅜" (1 cm) from folds.

2 ...... Press under 2" (5 cm) on one short end of the boxing strip. Lap the boxing strip over the zipper strip to cover zipper tab. Stitch through all layers 1½" (3.8 cm) from folded edge of boxing strip.

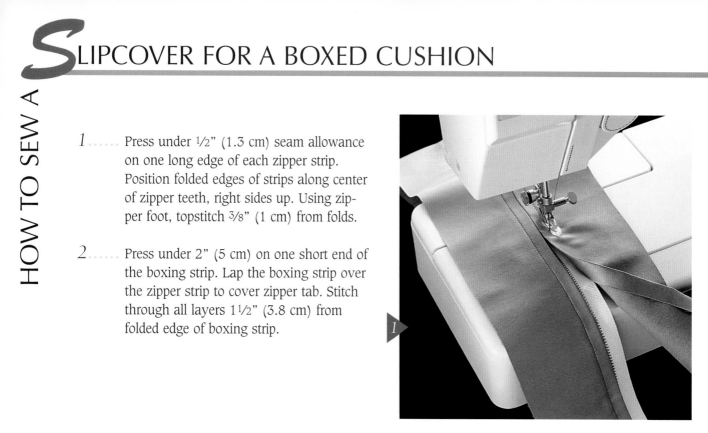

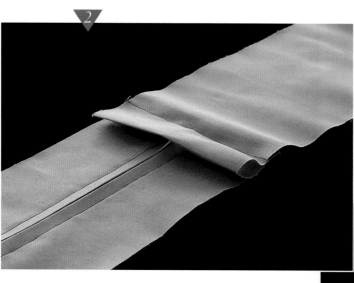

3 ...... Make and apply plain welting as on page 43, steps 1 to 5, or other trim as desired. Stitch welting to right side of top and bottom pieces.

4 ..... Place boxing strip on slipcover top, right sides together; center zipper on back edge. Start stitching 2" (5 cm) from zipper end, crowding cording. Clip corners as you come to them; stop stitching 4" (10 cm) from starting point.

5 ..... Clip to mark seam allowances at ends of boxing strip. Stitch boxing strip ends together. Trim excess fabric; finger-press seam open. Finish stitching boxing strip to slipcover top.

6 ..... Fold boxing strip, and clip seam allowance to mark lower corners; be sure all corners are aligned with corners on slipcover top. Open zipper.

HOW TO PREPARE THE

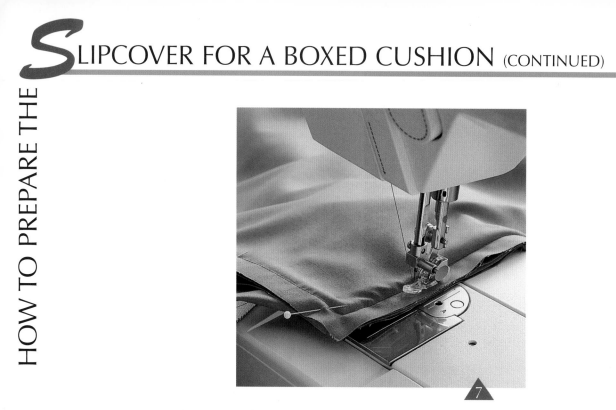

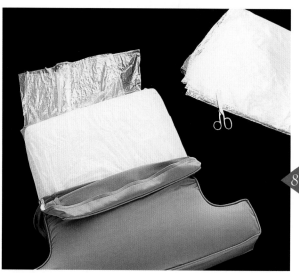

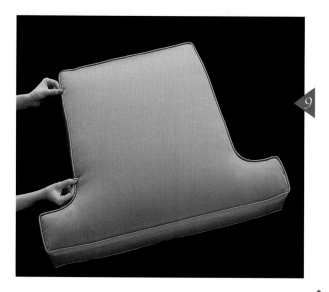

7 ...... Place boxing strip and slipcover bottom right sides together. Match clips of boxing strip to corners of slipcover bottom; stitch. Turn right side out.

8 ...... Fold cushion to insert it into slipcover. If necessary, wrap cushion with plastic to help slide it into slipcover; then remove plastic.

9 ...... Stretch cover from front to back. Close zipper. Smooth cushion from center to edges. Stretch welting taut from corner to corner to square the cushion.

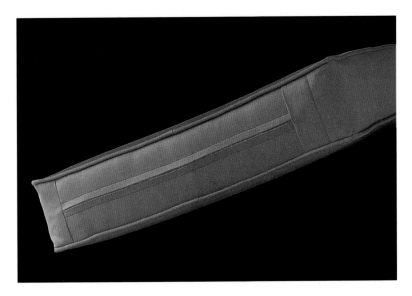

Alternative zipper placement. Install zipper across the back of slipcover, without extending it around the sides, if slipcover will be exposed on three sides.

HOW TO MATCH A PATTERNED FABRIC ON A BOXED CUSHION

1 ..... Cut slipcover top and boxing strip so pattern matches at front seamlines. Notch front corners on upper and lower edges of boxing strip.

2 ..... Stitch boxing strip to front edge of slipcover top first. Then continue stitching boxing strip to slipcover top and bottom.

Decorative
WELTING

Just as piping is used in garments to outline a fashion detail, welting is used in home decorator sewing to define or finish seams. Welting is fabric-covered cording, sewn into a seam to provide extra strength and a decorative finishing touch. Welting is the term used in upholstery and home decorating, and piping is the fashion term; however, the two terms are often interchanged.

Fabric strips for welting may be cut on the bias or the straight grain. For more economical use of the fabric, they are cut on the straight grain. Straight-grain welting is preferred for fabrics that are not tightly woven because bias welting can stretch too much, resulting in an uneven, wavy appearance.

For firm fabrics that must be shaped around curves, bias welting works better than straight-grain welting because it does not wrinkle. Bias welting strips do not have to be cut on the true bias. Cutting the strips at an angle less than 45° gives the flexibility of bias grain but requires less yardage. For stripes and plaids, bias welting does not require matching.

Cording with a diameter of 5/32" (3.8 mm) is the usual cording for pillows, cushions, and slipcover seams. Cut the fabric strips 1 1/2" (3.8 cm) wide. Cording with a diameter of 8/32" (6 mm) is slightly larger for similar applications. Cut the fabric strips 1 3/4" (4.5 cm) wide. To determine how wide to cut the fabric strips on other sizes of cording, wrap a piece of fabric or paper around the cording. Pin it together, encasing the cording. Cut 1/2" (1.3 cm) from the pin. Measure the width, and cut strips to match.

HOW TO MAKE AND ATTACH *W*ELTING

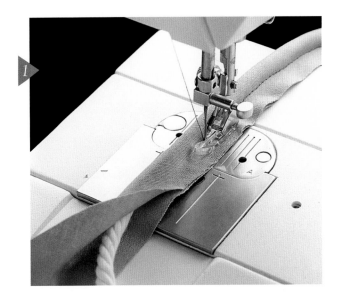

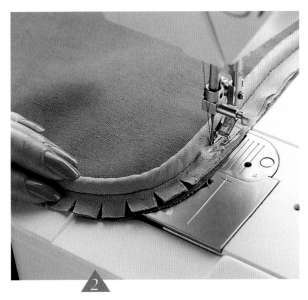

1 . . . . . . Center cording on wrong side of strip. Fold strip over cording, aligning raw edges. Using zipper foot on right side of needle, machine-baste close to cording.

2 . . . . . . Attach welting on right side with raw edges aligned. Begin stitching 2" (5 cm) from end of welting; stitch on bastestitching line. To ease at rounded corners, clip seam allowances to bastestitching.

3 . . . . . . Stop stitching 2" (5 cm) from point where cording ends will meet. Leaving needle in fabric, cut off one end of cording so it overlaps the other end by 1" (2.5 cm).

4 . . . . . . Remove 1" (2.5 cm) of stitching from each end of welting. Trim cording ends so they just meet.

5 . . . . . . Fold under ½" (1.3 cm) of overlapping fabric. Lap it around the other end; finish stitching.

Slipcovers
FOR WING CHAIRS

The basic instructions for slipcovering a wing chair are the same as for the fitted slipcover shown on page 14, with a few modifications for the wings of the chair. The wing chair slipcover is designed with a center back button and buttonhole closure in place of the corner zipper used in the fitted slipcover. If you prefer a zipper, simply follow the zipper directions for the fitted slipcover.

Many wing chairs have exposed legs that are decorative, and you may wish to leave them exposed. If the legs are decorative or protrude away from the chair, making a long skirt unsuitable, make a short gathered skirt as for the ruffled stool cover on page 107 or a short box-pleated skirt. A box-pleated skirt may be made self-lined, or for heavier fabric, it may be a single layer of fabric with a 1" (2.5 cm) double-fold hem. For a box-pleated skirt, determine the desired placement of pleats along the lower edge of the chair, the desired distance between pleats, and the desired depth of each pleat when calculating the cut width of the skirt piece on page 47.

LIST *of* MATERIALS

- ▶ Muslin, for pin-fitting the pieces.
- ▶ Decorator fabric.
- ▶ Contrasting fabric for welting, if desired.
- ▶ Cording for welting; select soft, pliable cording with a cotton core.
- ▶ Zipper, about 8" (20.5 cm) longer than back edge of cushion.
- ▶ Upholstery batting, if necessary, to pad the existing furniture.
- ▶ Polyurethane foam, 2" (5 cm) strips to insert at the sides and back of deck.
- ▶ T-pins, tacks or heavy-duty stapler and staples, for securing tacking strip to furniture.
- ▶ Button kit and six to seven buttons, for covered buttons, or six or seven decorative buttons.

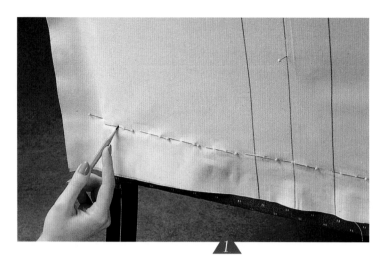

1...... Pin-fit the pattern for the inside and outside back as on page 17, steps 1 and 2; in step 1, mark a line 2" (5 cm) to the right and left of center, for overlap and under-lap at back center opening and, in step 2, cut muslin 8" (20.5 cm) wider, not 15" (38 cm). Mark line for upper edge of skirt.

2...... Measure the length of the inside wing from the seamline at the top to the seam-line at the top of the arm, and measure the width of the inside wing from the inside back across the wing at the widest point around the front to the seamline; add to this measurement the distance from the inside back to the outside back, measured across the top of the chair at the inside wing. Cut muslin about 6" (15 cm) wider and about 4" (10 cm) longer than measure-ments. Mark lengthwise grainline on inside wing piece, following lengthwise grain.

3...... Measure the length of the outside wing from the seamline at the top to the seam-line along the arm, and measure the width of the wing across the widest point. Cut muslin about 4" (10 cm) wider and longer than measurements. Mark lengthwise grainline on outside wing piece.

4...... Pin inside back piece to chair. Follow step 4 on page 17, omitting reference to clip-ping along arms and sides. Continue to mark line on inside back piece at top of chair along seamline of inside back and wing, and clip to marked line at point where top of chair meets inside back.

5...... Pin outside wing piece in place, with grainline perpendicular to floor and with lower edge extending ½" (1.3 cm) beyond seamline align-ing with arm. Smooth fabric upward; pin. Pin outside wing to outside back; mark seam.

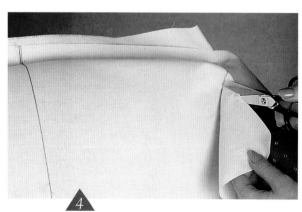

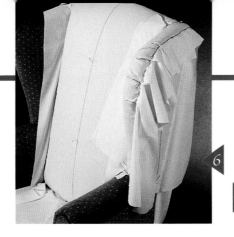

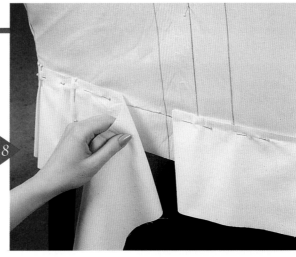

6 ..... Pin inside wing in place, with grainline perpendicular to floor and with lower edge extending ½" (1.3 cm) beyond seamline along arm. Push fabric into crevice at inside back; mark seamline and clip as in step 4. Pin inside back to outside back. Pin inside wing to outside wing at front; clip and trim fabric at lower edge as necessary for smooth fit. Pleat out excess fabric around curve of inside wing piece, duplicating pleats in existing fabric. Mark foldlines of pleats. Mark all seamlines on pinned edges.

7 ..... Follow steps 1 to 6 on pages 18 and 19 for a chair with a pleated arm; in step 4, make tucks, if necessary at back of arm where arm meets wing. Or follow steps 1 to 4 on page 20, for an arm with a front section.

8 ..... Follow page 21, steps 1 to 4, to pin-fit pattern for deck. Pin-fit skirt as on page 22, step 1; add 5" (12.5 cm) to each end of skirt to allow for overlap, underlap, facings, and seam allowances at center back closure and omit reference to seam at back corner for zipper. Follow page 22, step 2; if chair does not have a skirt, pin skirt slipcover piece to chair at marked upper skirt line, pinning ½" (1.3 cm) from upper raw edge of skirt.

9 ..... Follow page 23, step 1. Remove muslin. True marked lines on sides of inside back piece. Insert ruler into crevice at top of chair at side of inside back; record measurement for tuck-in. Repeat at center and bottom along side of inside back. On sides of inside back piece, mark points a distance from marked line equal to tuck-in measurement at top, center, and bottom. Draw line connecting points. Mark points along inside wing and inside arm pieces, corresponding to tuck-in points marked on inside back. Draw line connecting points.

10 .... On outside back, cut on marked line 2" (5 cm) to the right of centerline; discard remaining portion of outside back piece. Follow pages 23 and 24, steps 3 to 6; in step 3, mark ½" (1.3 cm) seam allowances at ends, and mark foldlines 3½" (9 cm) from ends for center back facings. Continue as on page 25, steps 8 and 9.

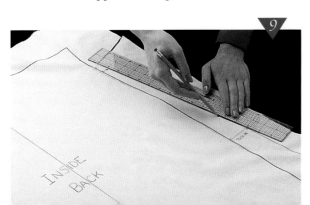

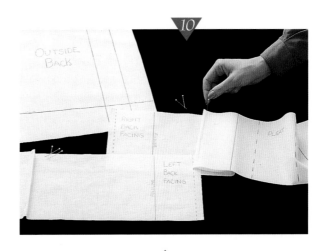

SLIPCOVER FOR A WING CHAIR WITH A PLEATED ARM

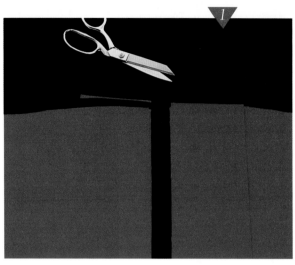

1...... Lay out and cut fabric for slipcover as on pages 26 to 28, cutting a right and left back piece, using the outside back pattern. Cut two facing strips for center back with length equal to measurement of line at center back and width equal to 4" (10 cm). Align long edges of facing strips with long edge of outside back, and trim upper edge of facing strips to match outer back piece.

2...... Apply welting to upper and front edges of outside arm, if desired, pivoting at corner. Follow page 30, steps 2 and 3. Pin the pleats in place around the inside wing. Check fit over wing of chair. Baste in place on seamline.

3...... Staystitch inside arm piece around curve at top of arm scant ½" (1.3 cm) from raw edges; clip to stitching. Apply welting to seam, if desired. Pin lower edge of inside wing to top of inside arm, right sides together; stitch from inside back to ½" (1.3 cm) from remaining side. Clip seam allowances.

4...... Stitch welting to outside wing piece around upper and front edges, if desired. Pin inside wing and arm piece to outside wing, right sides together; stitch around upper and front edges from seamline at back to lower raw edge at front.

5...... Follow pages 30 and 31, steps 4 to 6; in step 6, you will be pinning inside wings and inside arms to inside back on both sides. Apply interfacing to back facing pieces, within seam allowances. Press up ½" (1.3 cm) along one long edge of facing pieces. Apply welting to left outside back piece, if desired.

6 ..... Stitch facing pieces to outside back pieces, right sides together, using 1/2" (1.3 cm) seam allowances; press. Pin facing to outside back piece, wrong sides together; edge-stitch close to fold. Repeat for other piece. Lap left outside back piece over right outside back piece; baste across upper edges. Continue as on page 31, step 7, omitting reference to leaving seam open for zipper.

7 ..... Stitch skirt pieces together; press seams open. For self-lined skirt, fold skirt in half, right sides together. Stitch 1/2" (1.3 cm) from raw edges at ends; clip corners. Turn skirt right side out; fold in half lengthwise, wrong sides together, and press. Fold up 3" (7.5 cm) on each end of skirt for facing; press.

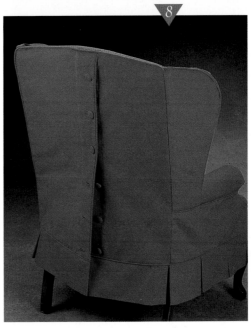

8 ..... Follow page 32, steps 9 and 10; in step 10, omit reference to zipper. Mark placement of buttonholes on left outside back piece, spacing evenly. Stitch buttonholes. Stitch buttons to right outside back piece at locations corresponding to buttonholes. Continue as on page 32, steps 11 and 12.

HOW TO SEW A $\mathcal{S}$LIPCOVER FOR A WING CHAIR WITH A FRONT ARM PIECE

1 ..... Follow step 1, opposite, for cutting and laying out slipcover. Pin the pleats in place around the inside wing. Check fit over wing of chair. Baste in place on seamline. Follow steps 3 and 4, opposite. Apply welting to upper edge of outside arm piece. Stitch horizontal seam, joining outside arm to inside arm. Pin and baste tucks at front edge of inside/outside arm. Apply welting to front edge of inside/outside arm.

2 ..... Follow page 33, steps 2 and 3. Complete vertical seam at front edge of outside arm. Follow page 31, step 6; you will be pinning inside wings and inside arms to inside back on both sides. Apply interfacing to back facing pieces, within seam allowances. Press up 1/2" (1.3 cm) along one long edge of facing pieces. Apply welting to left outside back piece, if desired. Complete slipcover as above, steps 6 to 8.

Semifitted
SLIPCOVERS

Use this versatile slipcover design to add new interest to a sofa or chair. This style slipcover works best on pieces that are straight across the center of the back and have rolled arms that are flush with the seat front. Rectangles of fabric are cut for each section of the chair or sofa and are fitted on the furniture; a separate muslin pattern is not used. Choose fabrics that can be railroaded for minimum seams. Or for fabrics with one-way designs, plan for a width of fabric across the center back of a sofa, and seam partial widths to each side. Box pleats are featured at each corner of the sofa and at the center back. The semifitted slipcover cushions are made as on pages 36 to 41.

For design detail, cording or fabric ties can be laced through grommets at the corners and center back of the slipcover. Or for a romantic look, use large bows, such as the ones shown below. This slipcover features a 1" (2.5 cm) double-fold hem and is designed to meet the floor.

Coordinating trims decorate the corners of these semifitted slipcovers. Cording inserted through grommets accents the sofa cover opposite. A bow adds a romantic touch to the slipcover below.

SEMIFITTED SLIPCOVER

LIST *of* MATERIALS

▶ Decorator fabric.

▶ One zipper for each seat or back cushion, about 8" (20.5 cm) longer than back edge of any seat cushion and about 8" (20.5 cm) longer than lower edge of any back cushion.

▶ Cording for welting, optional; select soft pliable cording with a cotton core.

▶ 7/16" (1.2 cm) grommets and grommet tool, optional, for design detail at corners and center back of slipcover.

CUTTING DIRECTIONS

For the front skirt and deck piece, measure the height and depth from the floor to the inner back along the line marked (**a**). To this measurement, add 3½" (9 cm) for the tuck-in at the back plus 2" (5 cm) for a 1" (2.5 cm) double-fold hem plus ½" (1.3 cm) for the back seam allowance. To determine the width of the front skirt and deck piece, measure the distance between the centers of the arms on the line marked (b) and also measure the length of the sofa along the skirt on the line marked (c), and use the longer of these two measurements. To this measurement, add 11" (28 cm) to allow for two 5" (12.5 cm) corner pleats and two ½" (1.3 cm) seam allowances. Cut one rectangle to these measurements. Label rectangle on wrong side of fabric, using a chalk pencil.

For the inner back, measure the height from a point where the top of the sofa meets the back down to the deck on the line marked (**d**). To this measurement add 3½" (9 cm) for the tuck-in at the back plus 1" (2.5 cm) for two ½" (1.3 cm) seam allowances. Measure the width of the inner back from the point where the side meets the back above the arm on one side to the same location on the other side of the sofa along the line marked (**e**). To this measurement, add 11" (28 cm) to allow for two 5" (12.5 cm) corner pleats and two ½" (1.3 cm) seam allowances. Cut one rectangle to these measurements. Label rectangle on wrong side of fabric, using a chalk pencil.

For the arm, measure the length from the deck on the inside of the arm, over the arm to the floor on the outside of the arm along the line marked (**g**); do not follow the contours of the arm on the outside. To this measurement, add 3½" (9 cm) for tuck-in at the deck plus 2" (5 cm) for a 1"

(2.5 cm) double-fold hem plus ½" (1.3 cm) for inside arm seam allowance. Measure the width from the center of the arm at the front along the arm to the point where the arm meets the back along the line marked (**h**). To this measurement, add 11" (28 cm) to allow for two 5" (12.5 cm) corner pleats and two ½" (1.3 cm) seam allowances. Cut two rectangles to these measurements. Label rectangles on wrong side of fabric, using a chalk pencil.

For the back, measure the height from a point where the top of the sofa meets the back down to the floor along the line marked (**i**). To this measurement, add 2" (5 cm) for a 1" (2.5 cm) double-fold hem plus ½" (1.3 cm) for the seam allowance at the top. Measure the width across the back between the widest points along the line marked (**j**). To this measurement, add 20" (51 cm) for a center back box pleat plus 11" (28 cm) to allow for two 5" (12.5 cm) corner pleats and two ½" (1.3 cm) seam allowances. Cut one rectangle to these measurements. Label rectangle on wrong side, using a chalk pencil.

For the underlay of the front corner pleats, cut two rectangles of fabric, with length equal to measurement from floor to deck (measurement (**f**) in the diagram, opposite) plus 2" (5 cm) for 1" (2.5 cm) double-fold hems plus ½" (1.3 cm) for seam allowance and width equal to 11" (28 cm). For the underlay of the back corner pleats, cut two rectangles of fabric, with length equal to the measurement from the floor at the back corner to the lower edge of the arm (measurement (**k**) in the diagram, opposite) plus 2" (5 cm) for 1" (2.5 cm) double-fold hems plus ½" (1.3 cm) for seam allowances.

DIAGRAM OF MEASUREMENTS

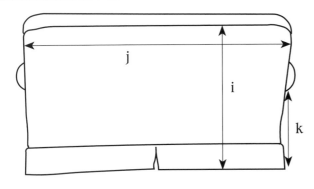

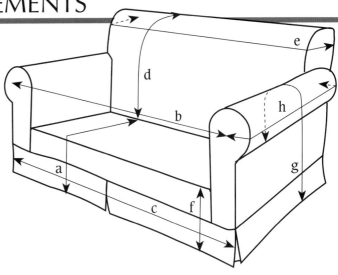

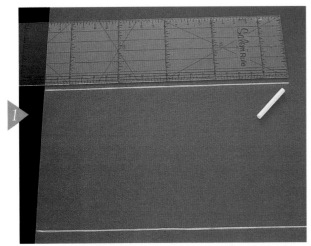

1...... Mark a chalk line 2" (5 cm) from one long side of front skirt and deck piece to mark hemline. Measure from the floor to the deck at the inside of the arm (measurement (f) in the diagram above), and mark about a 20" (51 cm) deck line parallel to and this distance from hemline on each side of front skirt and deck piece. Also chalk-mark centers of long sides.

2...... Position front skirt and deck piece on sofa, aligning center marks with center of sofa and hemline with floor. Fold up 4" (10 cm) at inner back for tuck-in and seam allowance. Mark sides of deck, using a chalk pencil. With 20" (51 cm) marked line aligned with deck and hemline aligned with floor, pin skirt portion of rectangle to sofa at corners and chalk-mark ends of sofa between marked chalk lines to mark foldline for corner pleats. Remove fabric rectangle from sofa.

3...... True marked lines, extending lines for sides of deck to raw edge at inner back and lines for pleat foldline to lower raw edge. Mark a point on raw edge at inner back, 4" (10 cm) from line for side of deck. Where line for side of deck and 20" (51 cm) marked front deck line intersect, mark a second point positioned ½"(1.3 cm) from each line. Draw line connecting points; this is the cutting line.

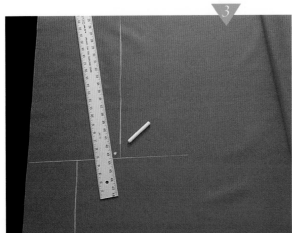

continued

4...... Mark cutting line ½" (1.3 cm) from 20" (51 cm) marked front deck line to where it intersects cutting line drawn in step 3. Mark cutting line 5½" (14 cm) from pleat foldline. Repeat to mark lines on other side. Cut on marked cutting lines.

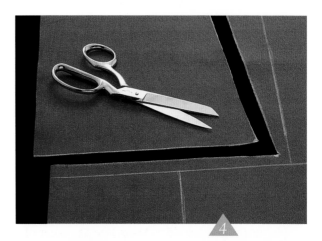

5...... Mark a chalk line 2" (5 cm) from one lower edge of arm piece to mark hemline. Measure from the floor to the deck at the inside of the arm (measurement (f) in the diagram on page 53) and mark about a 20" (51 cm) deck line parallel to and this distance from hemline on one side of arm piece. Mark a second line 3½" (9 cm) from raw edge at upper edge of fabric piece.

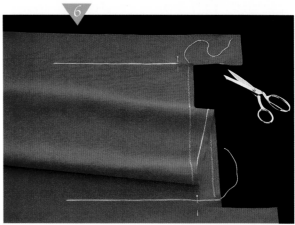

6...... Zigzag over a cord on wrong side of fabric 5" (12.5 cm) from side of rectangle between marked lines. Cut along marked 3½" (9 cm) line and ½" (1.3 cm) below marked 20" (51 cm) deck line for about 6" (15 cm). Trim excess fabric ½" (1.3 cm) from cord; do not cut cord.

7...... Position arm fabric, wrong side out, over arm, aligning hemline with floor. Fold up 4" (10 cm) at inside of arm for tuck-in and seam allowance. Pull fabric around to center of arm front, and pull on cord to gather fabric around arm. Pin ½" (1.3 cm) seam allowances together at center of arm, matching raw edges at deck level.

8...... Concentrate gathers at center of arm, and pull arm fabric below center of arm straight, until lower raw edge of arm front is ½" (1.3 cm) below deck. At lower raw edge of arm front, pull fabric snugly around arm and pin out about 1" to 1½" (2.5 to 3.8 cm) of excess fabric; cut a little more along 3½" (9 cm) and ½" (1.3 cm) below 20" (51 cm) deck line, if necessary for fitting. Continue to pin from lower edge of arm front to center of arm, gradually tapering to ½" (1.3 cm) seam allowance at center of arm.

9 ...... Remove fabric from arm. Mark stitching line along pin marks. Stitch on marked line from lower edge to center. Try arm piece on sofa and check fit. Adjust gathers and restitch, if necessary. Position arm piece on sofa, right side out, and smooth fabric in place. Mark point on inside of arm on 3½" (9 cm) marked line where lower edge of arm front meets deck.

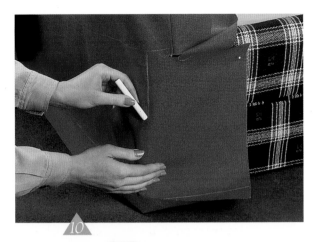

10 .... Fold excess fabric from side of arm around to front, over skirt. Mark line at corner of sofa, from 20" (51 cm) marked deck line to floor, to mark foldline for pleat. Remove arm piece from sofa. True marked line for pleat foldline, extending line to raw edge of fabric. Cut ½" (1.3 cm) below 20" (51 cm) marked deck line to pleat foldline. Mark a cutting line 5½" (14 cm) from pleat foldline. Cut on marked line.

11 .... Cut along 3½" (9 cm) marked line to point marked in step 9. Mark a cutting line on inside of arm piece from point on 3½" (9 cm) marked line to corner of fabric on opposite side. Cut on marked line.

12 .... Position arm piece over arm of sofa, and smooth in place; align hemline with floor, and align excess fabric at inside of arm so it tapers from 4" (10 cm) at the inner back to ½" (1.3 cm) at the front. Smooth fabric around curve where arm meets inner back. Chalk-mark a line along crevice in sofa from deck to top of arm. Smooth fabric around back, and continue to mark along crevice.

13 .... Remove fabric from arm, and true marked chalk line. Mark a point 4" (10 cm) from chalk line at inside of arm, and mark a point 2" (5 cm) from marked line at the remaining end of curved line. Draw a curved line connecting points. Cut on marked line.

continued

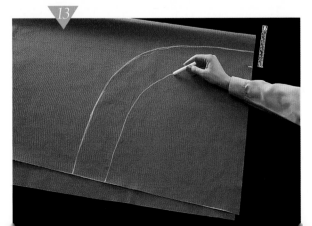

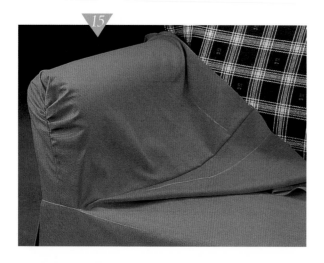

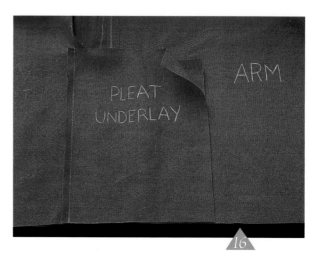

14 .... Press corner pleats of front deck and skirt section and arm piece along pleat foldlines. On front skirt and deck piece, staystitch scant ½" (1.3 cm) from raw edges at inside corners. Clip to stitching at corners.

15 .... Pin arm piece to deck and skirt piece along inner arm and front arm. Stitch ½" (1.3 cm) from raw edges, pivoting stitching at corner; begin stitching ½" (1.3 cm) from raw edge of inner back piece.

16 .... Pin length of pleat underlay to pleat of front skirt and deck piece, right sides together. Stitch ½" (1.3 cm) from raw edges. Pin opposite side of pleat underlay to pleat of arm piece, right sides together; pleat underlay will extend 1" (2.5 cm) above pleat of arm. Stitch along length of piece ½" (1.3 cm) from raw edges.

17 .... Pin upper edge of arm pleat to pleat underlay, with pleat underlay extending 1" (2.5 cm) above. Stitch ½" (1.3 cm) from upper edge of arm pleat, from long edge to pleat foldline. Fold pleat in place, and pin to front of arm.

18 .... Stitch in the ditch of the lower arm seamline from the corner of the inner arm to the center of the box pleat, catching the pleat in the stitching on the wrong side. Edgestitch along the front skirt pleat for about ½" (1.3 cm).

19 .... Mark seamline at upper edge of inner back piece ½" (1.3 cm) from long raw edge. Mark centers of long sides of inner back piece. Position inner back fabric over inner back of sofa, aligning seamline at upper edge along length of sofa where top and back of sofa meet. Fold up 4" (10 cm) at lower edge for tuck-in and seam allowance. Smooth fabric to sides.

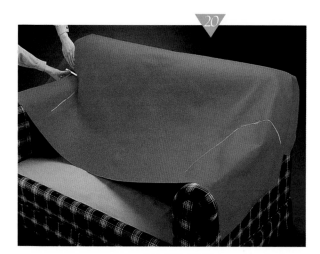

20 .... Chalk-mark lines along curves at sides of inner back piece where arms meet inner back. Wrap inner back fabric to back, and continue to chalk-mark line along crevice in sofa. Remove inner back piece, and true marked lines; continue lines to raw edges of fabric.

21 .... Mark a point on lower edge of inner back piece 4" (10 cm) from marked line. Mark a second point on side of inner back piece, 2" (5 cm) from other end of curved line. Draw a curved line, connecting points, as on page 55, step 13.

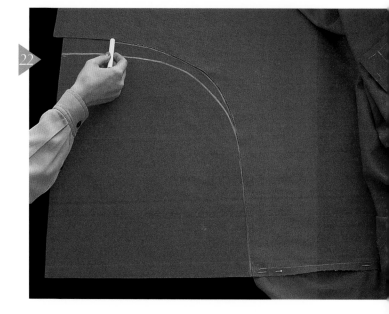

22 .... Place arm piece on inner back piece along curve, right sides together, aligning lower edge of inner back piece with lower edge of inner arm piece; fabric pieces may not meet at the remaining end of the curved line. Adjust curve of inner back piece to match inner arm piece. Cut on marked line. Repeat on other side.

23 .... Pin inner back piece to arm pieces and front skirt and deck piece, right sides together; pieces may not be the same length at end of curve around top of arm. Stitch ½" (1.3 cm) from raw edges.

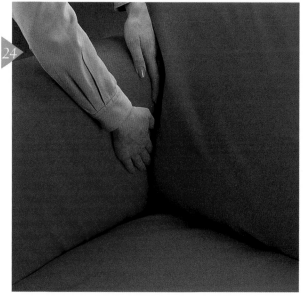

24 .... Position slipcover on sofa, aligning hemline with floor and aligning corner pleats with corners of sofa. Tuck in excess fabric around deck and in the crevices around inner arms.

continued

25 .... Pleat out excess fabric around curved ends of sofa on back side; secure with pins. Pleat out excess fabric around back of arms, if necessary; secure with pins. Mark seamline around back curve of sofa to lower edge of arm. Hand-baste pleats in place. Mark lines along back corners of sofa, from points just under arm to floor, to mark foldlines for pleats.

26 .... Remove slipcover from sofa. True seamline around pleats and foldlines for corner pleats. Draw line parallel to hemline from point where pleat foldline meets lower edge of arm to raw edge of fabric at side. Cut along marked line to within ½" (1.3 cm) from point where foldline meets lower edge of arm. Trim excess fabric around curve ½" (1.3 cm) from marked line. Draw line 5½" (14 cm) from pleat foldline. Cut on marked line.

27 .... Mark hemline 2" (5 cm) from lower edge of rectangle for back of slipcover. Mark center of upper long edge of rectangle for back of slipcover. Mark points on each side of center 5" (12.5 cm) and 10" (25.5 cm) from center. Fold 5" (12.5 cm) pleats at center to make box pleat; press. Baste across pleats at upper edge.

28 .... Pin back piece of fabric to back of sofa, aligning box pleat at center back, and aligning hemline with floor. Pin around corners. Mark corner seamlines with chalk to point where back meets lower edge of arm. Mark from this point to floor along corner to mark foldline for corner pleat. Remove slipcover back piece.

29 .... True seamline around corner curves, and pleat foldline, extending foldline to raw edge of fabric. Mark a line parallel to hem-line from point where foldline meets lower edge of arm to raw edge of fabric at side. Continue cutting as in step 26, opposite.

30 .... Pin pieced slipcover sections to back section along upper and side edges. Stitch around upper and side edges ½" (1.3 cm) from raw edges, stitching ½" (1.3 cm) beyond upper edges of inside pleats. Pin pleat underlay to upper and long side edges of inner pleat on arm and back piece. Stitch ½" (1.3 cm) from raw edges. Repeat on other side.

31 .... Stitch 1" (2.5 cm) double-fold hem around lower edge of slipcover. At seams inside fold of pleats, press seam allowance open for about 3½" (9 cm). Trim lower 2" (5 cm) of seam allowance to ¼" (6 mm). Fold up hem allowance, and stitch; clip seam allowance just above hem. Refold pleat, and press; edgestitch close to fold from hemline to clip in seam allowance. Make semifitted slipcovers for cushions as on page 37.

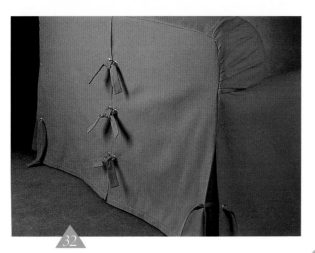

32 .... Make ties for front and back corners and center back of slipcover, if desired, as on page 83, step 4; stitch across both short ends of tie, and leave an opening on the center of one long side for turning. Install large grommets at corners of slipcover and at center back pleat, if desired, using grommet tool. Insert cording or tie-tabs through grommets, and tie as desired.

Simple
SLIPCOVERS

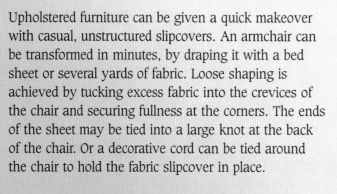

Upholstered furniture can be given a quick makeover with casual, unstructured slipcovers. An armchair can be transformed in minutes, by draping it with a bed sheet or several yards of fabric. Loose shaping is achieved by tucking excess fabric into the crevices of the chair and securing fullness at the corners. The ends of the sheet may be tied into a large knot at the back of the chair. Or a decorative cord can be tied around the chair to hold the fabric slipcover in place.

An armless chair can be draped gracefully with a length of decorator fabric and tied with a ribbon or cord at the back of the seat. Hems can be sewn, if desired, or neat, narrow selvages can be left exposed.

King-size sheet becomes an instant slipcover for an armchair. Excess fabric is tied out at the front corners and into a large, loose knot at the chair back.

LIST _of_ MATERIALS

▸ One flat king-size bed sheet.

▸ Cord or narrow grosgrain ribbon, for tying excess fullness at corners.

▸ Polyurethane foam, 2" (5 cm) thick, cut into three strips, 2" (5 cm) wide, with lengths equal to sides and back of seat cushion.

_1_ ...... Drape sheet over chair, with decorative sheet hem just above floor at front of chair and excess fabric width distributed evenly at sides.

_2_ ...... Tuck excess sheet fabric into crevices around seat cushion, until sheet reaches desired length at sides; smooth sheet over arms toward chair back. Insert foam strips into crevices to help hold sheet in place.

_3_ ...... Tie excess sheet fabric at back of chair into large knot, keeping grain of the sheet hanging parallel to floor at sides of chair.

_4_ ...... Tie out excess fullness at front corners on underside of slipcover, using cording or ribbon.

SIMPLE SLIPCOVERS
WITH DECORATOR FABRIC

LIST *of* MATERIALS

- 6 to 7 yd. (5.5 to 6.4 m) fabric, 54" to 60" (127 to 152.5 cm) wide, depending on size of chair; select fabric with solid color or nondirectional print.
- Polyurethane foam, 2" (5 cm) thick, cut into three strips, 2" (5 cm) wide, with lengths equal to sides and back of seat cushion.
- Twist pins, optional.
- Decorative cord, with length equal to circumference of chair plus additional length for tying knot.

Decorator fabric, cut into two lengths, is draped sideways over the seat and back of an armchair. Excess fabric is tucked around the cushion and folded out at the chair back. Decorative cord adds a finishing touch.

SLIPCOVER AN ARMCHAIR WITH FABRIC

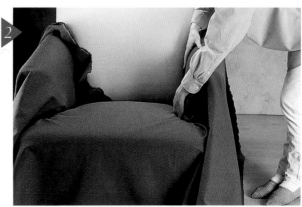

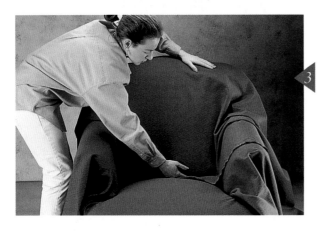

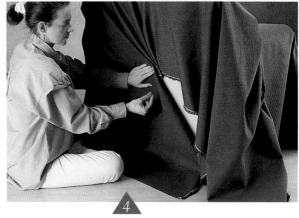

1 ..... Cut the fabric into two equal lengths. Drape one length of fabric horizontally over seat and arms of the chair; turn under selvage, and puddle the fabric slightly on floor at front of chair, with excess fabric length distributed evenly at sides.

2 ..... Tuck excess fabric into the crevices at sides and back of seat cushion, until desired amount of fabric puddles on floor at the sides; smooth fabric over the arms toward chair back.

3 ..... Drape second length of fabric horizontally over back of the chair, tucking 6" to 10" (15 to 25.5 cm) into the crevice at back of seat cushion; allow fabric to fall straight down at the sides, overlapping front of the slipcover and puddling on the floor.

4 ..... Fold out the excess fabric diagonally at back of the chair, overlapping folds and allowing the excess length to puddle on the floor. Secure to the chair back, using twist pins, if desired.

5 ..... Insert foam strips into crevices around cushion to hold the fabric in place. Tie decorative cord tightly around chair, parallel to floor, just below cushion. Arrange excess fullness into gathered clusters under cord at corners of chair.

SIMPLE SLIPCOVERS FOR ARMLESS SIDE CHAIRS

LIST *of* MATERIALS

▸ Fabric, 45" to 60" (115 to 152.5 cm) wide, depending on size of chair.

▸ Ribbon or decorative cord.

CUTTING DIRECTIONS

Cut the fabric with the length equal to the continuous distance from the floor up to the front of the chair, over the seat to the back, and up and over the back to the floor plus 2" (5 cm) for the hems.

Armless side chairs are draped from front to back with decorator fabric. Brocade ribbons, secured at the backs of the seats, hold the slipcovers in place.

HOW TO SLIPCOVER AN *A*RMLESS CHAIR

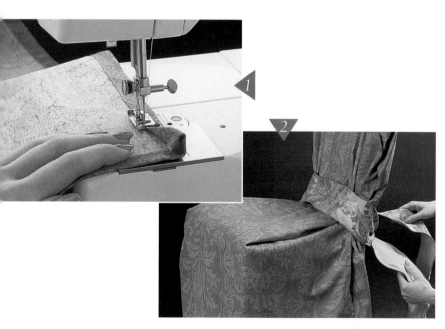

1 ...... Press cut end under ½" (1.3 cm) twice; stitch to make double-fold hem. Repeat for opposite end. Trim selvages and hem long sides, if necessary.

2 ...... Drape fabric over the chair, smoothing the fabric to the back of the seat, with hemmed ends at the floor. Tuck in the excess fullness at the back of the chair. Wrap ribbon or cord around chair and fabric at back of the seat; knot securely at the chair back.

MORE IDEAS FOR *Simple* SLIPCOVERS

Sofa slipcover is made from two flat queen-size sheets sewn together in the center. Make the slip-cover following steps 2 and 4 on page 62, knotting excess at all corners as in step 3.

*Shimmery organza is used to slipcover an
ornate metal side chair, creating an alluring
translucent look. Excess fabric is knotted
gracefully at the back.*

Slipcovers
FOR FOLDING CHAIRS

Slipcovers for folding chairs are an easy and affordable way to dress up an old steel folding chair. For special occasions, for a change of seasons, or simply for some fun in home decorating, folding-chair slipcovers are attractive and versatile. They can work with any decorating scheme from contemporary to country, depending upon fabric choice and styling options. And they offer a practical solution to the age-old problem posed by large gatherings: attractive yet portable and stowable temporary seating.

Folding chairs come in a variety of shapes and sizes, quite similar but not exactly the same. To make a well-fitting slipcover, make a custom-fitted pattern out of muslin. Start with four rectangles of fabric cut approximately to size, then drape and pin them to the chair to fine-tune the shape. Once this muslin has been fitted, use it as a pattern for cutting the slipcover.

When you make the actual slipcover, add a decorative bow tied across the back, or add contrasting welting or ruffles or creative touches of your own.

LIST *of* MATERIALS

- ▶ 3 yd. (2.75 m) unbleached muslin, 42" (107 cm) wide, for pattern.
- ▶ Folding chair.
- ▶ Marker or pencil, pins, shears, double-stick tape.
- ▶ Heavy weight, such as books or gallon (3.78 L) bottle of water.
- ▶ Decorator fabric.

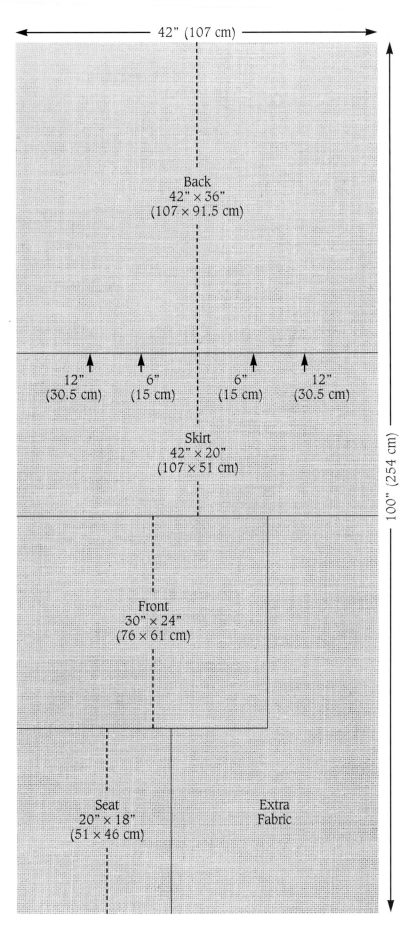

42" (107 cm)

Back
42" × 36"
(107 × 91.5 cm)

12"
(30.5 cm)

6"
(15 cm)

6"
(15 cm)

12"
(30.5 cm)

Skirt
42" × 20"
(107 × 51 cm)

Front
30" × 24"
(76 × 61 cm)

Seat
20" × 18"
(51 × 46 cm)

Extra
Fabric

100" (254 cm)

Muslin pattern layout. Mark muslin for rough pattern pieces; cut on solid lines. Mark dotted centerlines. Mark arrows on skirt pattern piece, 6" (15 cm) and 12" (30.5 cm) on each side of centerline.

1 ...... Pin back and front pattern pieces together for 4" (10 cm) on either side of the center marks. Pin horizontally from center toward sides, using a ½" (1.3 cm) seam allowance.

2 ...... Drape pinned pattern over chair, matching centerlines to center of chair back. Secure pattern at top of chair back with double-stick tape. Tuck pattern under back legs; keep grainline straight.

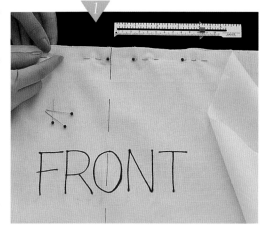

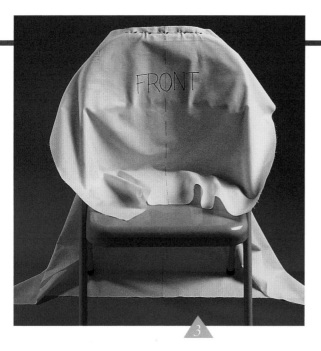

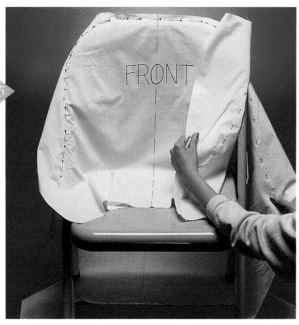

3...... Push front pattern piece toward back edge of seat at bottom to allow enough ease for sitting. Secure pattern to chair with double-stick tape at center of seat and both corners.

4...... Drape back pattern around curve of chair. Drape smoothly, keeping grainline perpendicular to floor. Pin along edge of chair to indicate seamline. Repeat for other side.

5...... Drape front pattern around curve of chair. Pin along edge of chair to indicate seamline. Pin back pattern to front pattern along seamlines, adjusting to fit chair smoothly and maintain grainline.

6...... Trace edge of the chair seat at bottom of front pattern. Trim to 1" (2.5 cm) beyond the traced outline.

continued

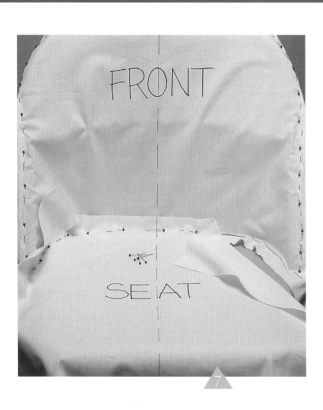

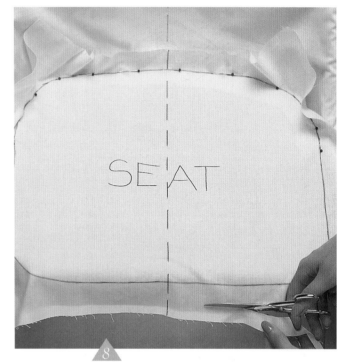

7...... Secure the seat pattern to the chair at center front with double-stick tape. Pin back of seat pattern to bottom of front pattern, stopping where the front and back pieces meet.

8...... Trace the outline of chair seat onto seat pattern. Add ¼" (6 mm) to front edge of seat pattern to allow for the rounded front edge of chair. Trim to 1" (2.5 cm) beyond outline.

9...... Gather or pleat skirt pattern between 6" and 12" (15 and 30.5 cm) marks on each side of centerline. Draw up each set of gathers to 3" (7.5 cm).

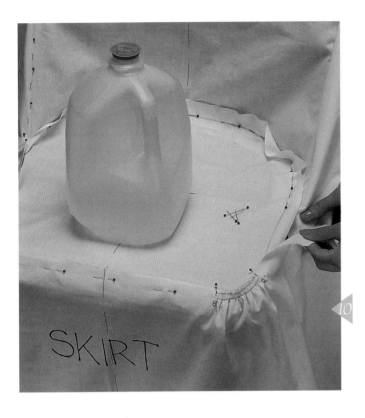

10.... Weight pattern pieces on chair so they do not move; a gallon (3.78 L) of water or stack of books works well. Match center-lines of seat and skirt patterns. Pin skirt to seat ending where all four pieces meet.

11.... Turn up and pin hem to the desired length. Pin skirt to back pattern at sides. Examine fit of muslin on chair and make any necessary adjustments. Pattern should fit snugly, without pulling.

12.... Mark seamlines between pins on all pieces. Mark placement for gathers on seat and skirt patterns. Mark all pieces with an "X" at point where all four pat-tern pieces meet at sides.

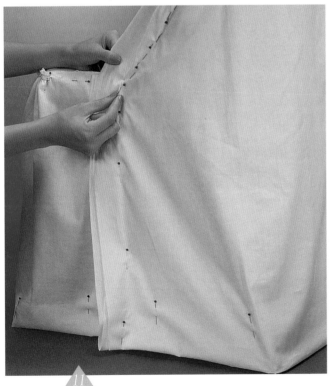

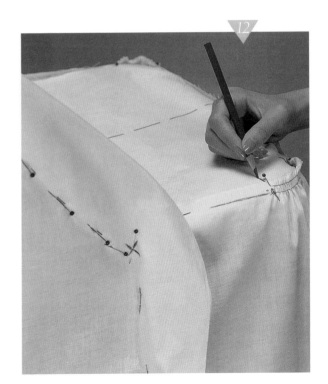

continued

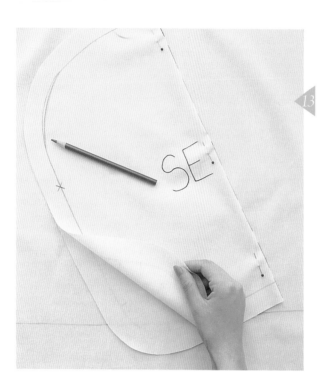

13.... Remove pins and release gathers. Lay pieces flat. Mark seamlines. Fold pieces along centers. Compare markings on each half. Make any necessary adjustments so pattern is symmetrical.

14.... Trim the hem allowance on the skirt to 2" (5 cm) for a finished 1" (2.5 cm) double-fold hem.

15.... Repin, and try pattern on chair. Adjust the fit, seamlines, and placement marks, as necessary. Add ½" (1.3 cm) seam allowances; trim excess fabric. Try pattern on chair again, if desired.

16.... Cut chair cover from decorator fabric using the muslin pieces as a pattern. Transfer markings.

17.... Cut two pieces for ties, each 7" (18 cm) wide and 42" (107 cm) long. Fold in half lengthwise, rights sides together. Fold one end to form triangle; cut on fold. Stitch cut side and bias end; turn and press.

18.... Stitch front to seat along back edge of seat between Xs (a). Stitch back to skirt at side seams, inserting tie in seam (b). Gather skirt between markings. Pin front and seat to back and skirt (c). Stitch hem.

PARTIAL COVER-UPS

FRESH & CAREFREE

Slipcovers
FOR KITCHEN & DINING CHAIRS

Two-piece slipcovers can be used on simple kitchen or dining room chairs to update a look or to help soften the room with fabric. Slipcovers can also be used to cover up worn or unmatched chairs. Slipcover styles can range from country to formal, depending on the fabric choice and detailing of the chair. Both the back and the seat slipcovers are lined for durability and body. Welting, applied around the seat slipcover and along the lower edge of the back slipcover, adds a finishing touch.

The back slipcover and the skirt on the chair seat can be long or short. When determining the desired back length and skirt length of the slip-covers, take into account the style and detailing of the chair. For a nice drape and an attractive appearance, make the skirt at least 5" to 6" (12.5 to 15 cm) long and end the skirt slightly above or below any cross pieces of the chair. Chairs with seats that slope toward the back will have skirts that also slope toward the back, making the fabric hang slightly off-grain at the side back of the chair. For this reason, avoid long skirt styles on chairs that have sloping seats. It may also be desirable to avoid fabrics with obvious stripes, plaids, or one-way designs on chairs of this style.

The seat slipcover can be made with either pleats or clustered gathers at the front corners. Select chairs with an open back at the edge of the seat to allow decorative ties to be secured to the back posts. Concealed twill-tape ties secure the cover to the front legs of the chair.

For back slipcovers that are long, the back of the chair must be straight from the seat to the upper edge of the back or taper slightly inward; if the upper edge of the chair back is wider than the

lower edge, it will not be possible to slip the cover on. However, short slipcovers, covering one-third to one-half of the back, may be suitable for this style chair. You may want to test-fit a muslin pattern before purchasing the decorator fabric.

LIST of MATERIALS

▶ Muslin, for patterns.
▶ Decorator fabric.
▶ Lining fabric.
▶ 1" (2.5 cm) twill tape.
▶ 5/32" (3.8 mm) cording, for optional welting.

CUTTING DIRECTIONS

Make the seat and back patterns as on pages 80 to 82. Cut one seat each from outer fabric and lining; transfer the markings. For a gathered skirt, cut the fabric as on pages 82 and 83, steps 1 and 2. For a skirt with corner pleats, cut the fabric as on page 85, step 1. Cut eight fabric strips 1½" (3.8 cm) wide and 10" to 16" (25.5 to 40.5 cm) long for the back ties on the seat cover. Cut four 12" (30.5 cm) lengths of twill tape for the concealed front ties. Using the pattern for a straight or shaped slipcover back (pages 81 and 82), cut one front and one back from both the outer fabric and lining; transfer the markings.

If welting is desired, cut 1 5/8" (4 cm) bias strips. The combined length of the strips is equal to the circumference of the seat cover and the lower edge of the back cover; allow extra for seams and overlaps.

CHAIR SEAT SLIPCOVER PATTERN

HOW TO MAKE A

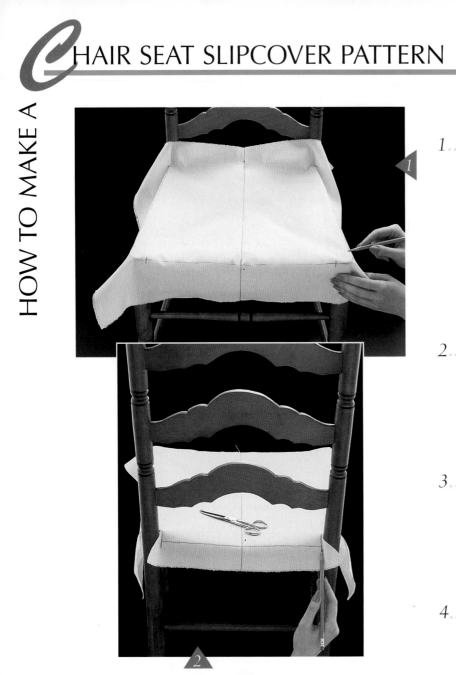

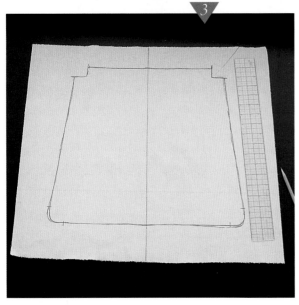

1 ...... Measure the chair seat; cut muslin about 6" (15 cm) larger than measurements. Mark the center line on lengthwise grain. Center muslin on seat; pin or tape in place. Using pencil, mark outer rim of seat front, and sides to back posts, rounding square corners slightly. Mark placement for front ties.

2 ...... Mark back edge of chair seat on muslin; clip the fabric as necessary for snug fit if seat is shaped around back posts. On muslin, mark the placement of skirt back between the chair posts.

3 ...... Remove muslin from the chair. Redraw seamlines as necessary, using a straightedge; redraw curved lines, drawing smooth curves. Reposition muslin on chair; adjust as necessary.

4 ...... Add ½" (1.3 cm) seam allowances. Cut pattern on marked lines.

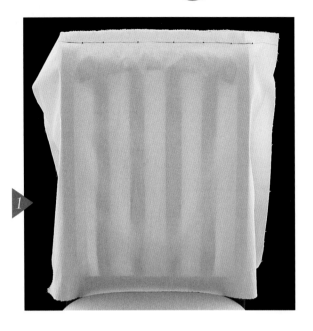

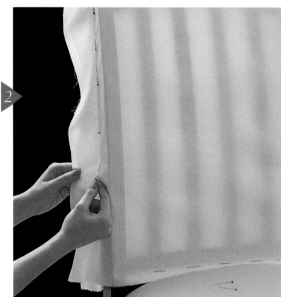

1 ...... *Straight upper edge.* Measure chair back; cut two pieces of muslin about 6" (15 cm) wider and 2" (5 cm) longer than measurements. Mark a line, 1" (2.5 cm) from raw edge, for upper edge of chair back; pin pieces together on the marked line. Center the muslin on the chair with the marked line at upper edge.

2 ...... Pin muslin at sides of chair, allowing ample ease. Mark desired finished length. Pull gently on cover to make sure it slides off easily; adjust width or length of cover, if necessary.

3 ...... Mark seamlines, following pin placement. Label patterns for front and back.

4 ...... Remove muslin from the chair. Redraw seamlines as necessary, using straightedge. Repin muslin, and position on chair; adjust as necessary. Front and back of pattern may be different sizes.

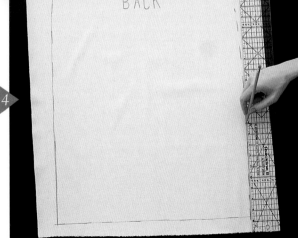

continued

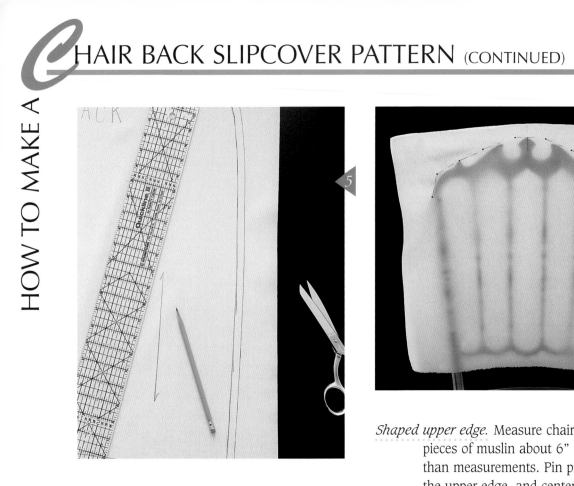

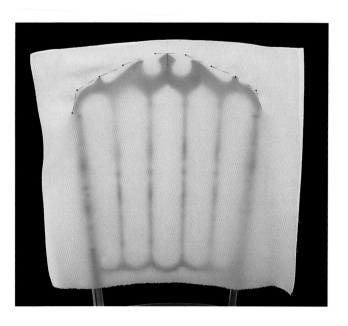

5 ...... Mark ½" (1.3 cm) seam allowances; mark grainline. Cut the pattern on marked lines.

Shaped upper edge. Measure chair back; cut two pieces of muslin about 6" (15 cm) larger than measurements. Pin pieces together at the upper edge, and center over chair back; adjust pins to follow contours of the chair, simplifying design as necessary. Continue as for chair back with straight upper edge, as on page 81, steps 2 to 4; in step 4, smooth any curved lines. Complete pattern as in step 5.

HOW TO SEW A CHAIR SEAT SLIPCOVER WITH GATHERED CORNERS

1 ...... Measure pattern seamline around the front and sides of seat between markings at the back posts; add 12" (30.5 cm) for the corner gathers plus 1" (2.5 cm) for seam allowances. Cut the fabric strip for front skirt to this length, piecing fabric, if necessary; width of strip is equal to twice the desired finished skirt length plus 1" (2.5 cm) for seam allowances.

Front skirt width:
46½" + 12" + 1" = 59½"
Front skirt length:
9"x2 + 1" = 19"

2...... Measure pattern seamline between markings for back skirt. Cut fabric strip for back skirt to this length plus 1" (2.5 cm); width of strip is equal to twice the desired finished skirt length plus 1" (2.5 cm) for seam allowances.

3...... Staystitch any inner corners and curves on chair seat top and lining. Clip to, but not through, stitching as necessary.

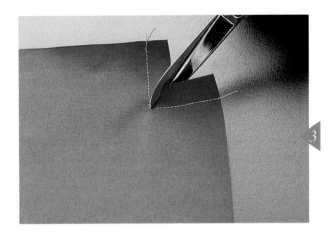

4...... Make welting, if desired, and apply to seat top as on page 43. Place two tab strips right sides together; stitch 1/4" (6 mm) seam around long sides and one short end of tab. Trim corners and turn right side out; press. Pin ties to the right side of seat top at back corners as desired, aligning raw edges.

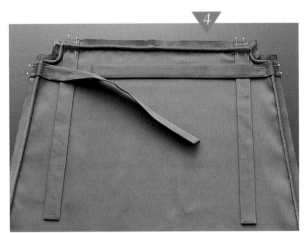

5...... Fold the skirt front in half lengthwise, right sides together; stitch 1/2" (1.3 cm) seams on short ends. Turn right side out; press. Repeat for skirt back.

6...... Pin-mark center of skirt at raw edges. Measure edge of seat pattern on seamline, from center front to corner; add 3" (7.5 cm). Measure this distance out from center of skirt, and pin-mark for corners. Clip-mark skirt 6" (15 cm) from both sides of corner pin marks.

continued

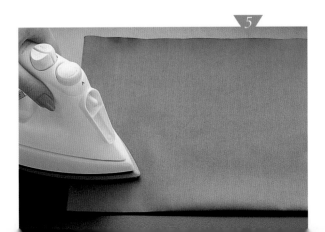

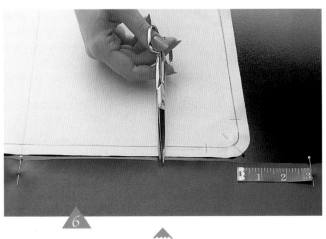

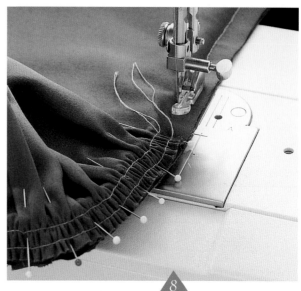

7...... Stitch two rows of gathering threads along upper edge of skirt front between clip marks, 1/4" (6 mm) and 1/2" (1.3 cm) from raw edges.

8...... Pin skirt front to the seat top, right sides together, matching the raw edges and markings for center front and corners. Pull gathering threads to fit. Machine-baste skirt to seat top, using zipper foot.

9...... Pin skirt back to the seat top, right sides together, matching the raw edges; stitch, using zipper foot.

10.... Pin or baste twill-tape ties to wrong side of skirt at front-corner tie markings.

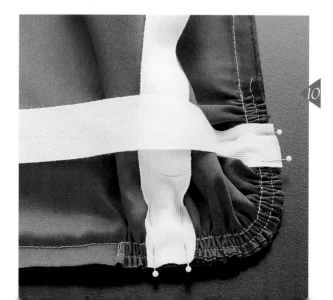

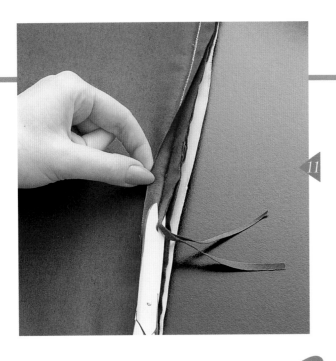

11 .... Pin skirt and ties to the seat to prevent catching them in seam allowance. Pin lining to the seat, with right sides together and raw edges even. Stitch, leaving a 6" (15 cm) center opening on back of seat. Trim seam allowances; clip curves and corners.

12 .... Turn the seat cover right side out; press. Slipstitch opening closed. Position seat cover on chair; secure the back ties in a bow or a square knot. Lift skirt, and secure front ties; trim excess length.

HOW TO SEW A *C*HAIR SEAT SLIPCOVER WITH CORNER PLEATS

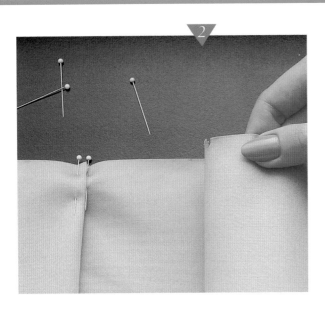

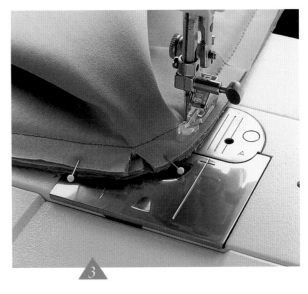

1 ...... Follow steps 1 to 5 on pages 82 and 83; in step 1, add 24" (61 cm) instead of 12" (30.5 cm). Pin-mark the center of the skirt at raw edges. Measure outer edge of seat pattern on seamline, from center front to corner, and add 6" (15 cm); measure this distance from center of skirt front, and pin-mark for corners. Clip-mark the fabric 6" (15 cm) from both sides of the corner pin marks.

2 ...... Fold 3" (7.5 cm) inverted pleats at front corners, matching the clip marks to the corner pin marks; press. Machine-baste the pleats in place.

3 ...... Pin the skirt front to the seat top, right sides together, matching raw edges and markings for center front and corners; clip skirt at the corners as necessary. Machine-baste skirt to seat top. Complete skirt as in steps 9 to 12, opposite.

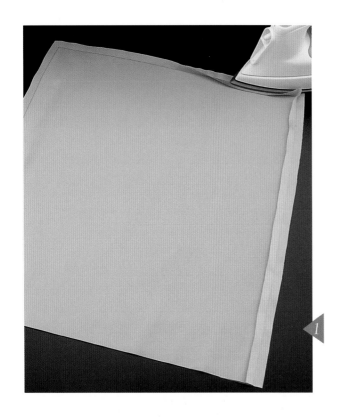

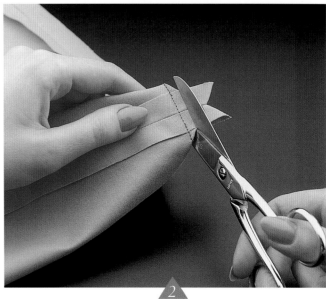

1 . . . . . . *Straight upper edge.* Place the front and the back outer fabric pieces right sides together, matching the raw edges. Stitch ½" (1.3 cm) seam around sides and upper edge. Press seam open.

2 . . . . . . To accommodate depth of chair, open out the corners, aligning seam allowances; stitch across corners, a distance equal to the depth of the chair. Trim seam.

3 . . . . . . Attach welting, if desired, to lower edge of outer cover as on page 43, steps 2 to 5. Stitch lining as for outer cover, leaving a 6" (15 cm) center opening on one side. Press seam allowances open.

4 ...... Place outer fabric and lining right sides together, matching lower edge; stitch ½" (1.3 cm) seam.

5 ...... Turn slipcover, lining side out, through the opening in the lining; press the lower edge. Slipstitch opening closed. Turn slipcover right side out; place over back of chair.

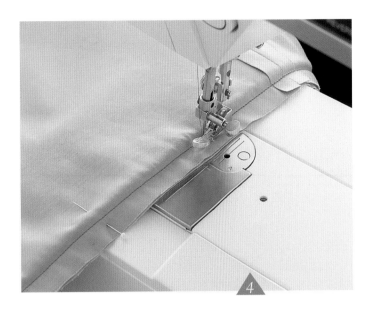

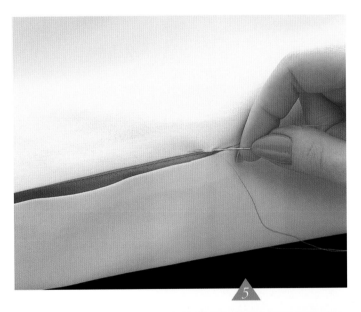

Shaped upper edge. Place the front and back outer fabric pieces right sides together, matching raw edges. Stitch ½" (1.3 cm) seam around sides and upper edge; press open. Trim seam; clip any curves. Complete as in steps 3 to 5, opposite.

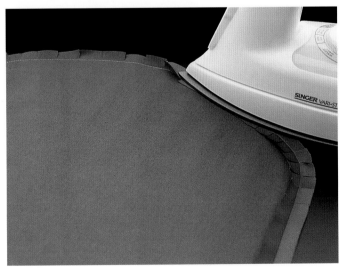

*Coordinating fabrics
are used to cover a pair of
unmatched porch chairs. One slipcover
has a skirt gathered to double fullness. The other
slipcover features a skirt with corner pleats. It has
additional welting around the sides and upper
edge of the chair back. The ties on both chair covers, made 4" (10 cm) wide, create the large bows.*

Grosgrain ribbon (left) provides contrast along the lower edges of this chair back and skirt. Apply the grosgrain ribbon by edgestitching along both sides.

Buttons (below) accent the pleats of the chair skirt and add detail to the lower edge of the back slipcover.

Reversible
SEAT COVERS

Freshen the look of dining room and kitchen chairs with simple seat covers. The lined cover is shaped at the front of the chair and secured to the chair with fabric ties at the back legs. To make the seat cover reversible, use a coordinating decorator fabric for the lining. For best results, choose firmly woven, mediumweight decorator fabrics. These fabrics wear well and are easy to work with. When working with heavier fabrics, select a lighter-weight fabric for the lining. To add a decorative touch to the cover, embellish the lower edge with a contrasting trim, such as ribbon or braid. This seat cover is suitable for armless chairs that have open backs and smooth, flat seats.

LIST *of* MATERIALS

- ▶ Muslin, for pattern.
- ▶ Decorator fabric.
- ▶ Lining fabric.
- ▶ Decorative trim, optional.

CUTTING DIRECTIONS

Make the seat cover pattern as on page 92. Cut one piece each from fabric and lining. Cut four fabric strips, 2" (5 cm) wide and 10" to 16" (25.5 to 40.5 cm) long, for ties.

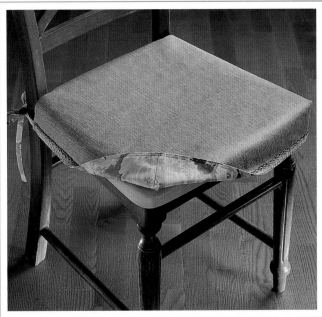

Seat covers can give an updated look to dining room and kitchen chairs. Make the covers reversible by using a decorator fabric for the lining, and, for added interest, embellish the lower edge with a decorative trim.

$\mathcal{S}$EAT COVER PATTERN

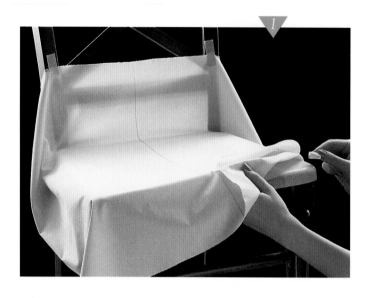

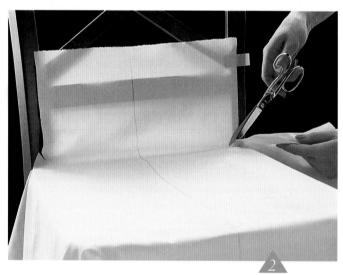

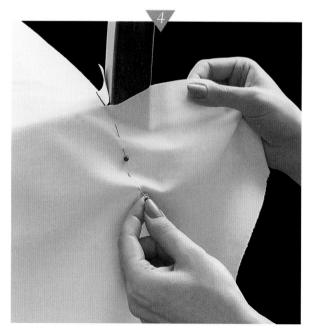

1 ...... Measure chair seat, and add 3" to 4" (7.5 to 10 cm) on all sides for drop length; cut a piece of muslin about 4" (10 cm) larger than measurements. Mark centerline, following lengthwise grain. Center the muslin on the seat; pin or tape in place.

2 ...... Clip fabric diagonally at back corners, so fabric fits around the back posts; make additional clips as necessary for smooth fit.

3 ...... Smooth fabric around sides and front of chair; pin out excess fabric at front corners. Mark seamline at front corners, using pencil.

4 ...... Mark seamline around the back posts, using pencil. Pin-mark ends of seat cover on drop, at sides of chair; repeat for drop at chair back.

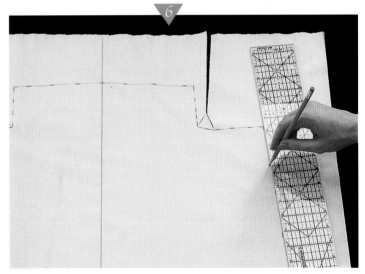

5...... Pin-mark the lower edge of cover at the desired length around front, sides, and back; drop length on sides and back should align. Mark the seamlines.

6...... Remove muslin from the chair. Redraw seamlines as necessary, using straightedge; redraw any curved lines, drawing smooth curves. Reposition muslin on chair; make corrections, if necessary.

7...... Add ½" (1.3 cm) seam allowances. Cut pattern on the marked lines.

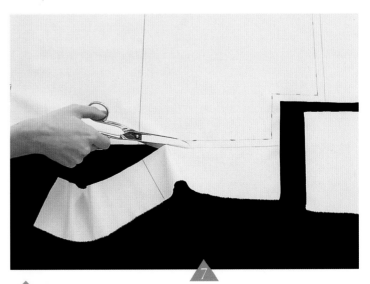

1 ...... Fold tie piece in half lengthwise;
stitch ¼" (6 mm) from long
edges and one short end. Trim
seam allowances and corners.
Turn right side out; press. Pin one
tie to right side of seat cover at
lower back corner, with raw edges
even and long stitched edge of the
tie ½" (1.3 cm) from lower edge
of the cover. Baste tie in place.
Repeat for remaining ties.

2 ...... Pin seam at front corners of seat
cover; stitch. Repeat for lining.
Press seams to one side, pressing
seams of the seat cover and the
lining in opposite directions.

3 ...... Pin lining to the seat cover, right
sides together and raw edges
even. Stitch ½" (1.3 cm) seam,
leaving 6" (15 cm) opening, centered on back of seat cover.

4...... Trim outside corners diagonally;
clip any curves and inside corners.
Press seam allowances open.

5...... Turn cover right side out; press.
Slipstitch opening closed. Position
trim, if desired, at the lower edge
of the cover or lining, using glue
stick. Turn under ½" (1.3 cm) at
ends. Topstitch trim in place;
stitch both sides in same direction
to prevent diagonal wrinkles.

6...... Position seat cover on chair;
secure ties in bow or square knot.

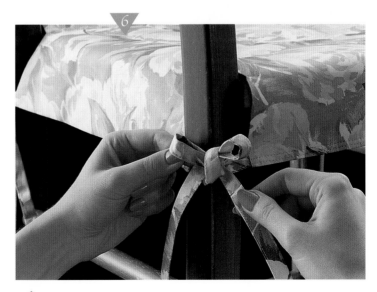

Table topper is used for an ottoman slipcover. The corners of the table topper are tied to the ottoman legs, using decorative cord. Large tassels add an elegant touch.

Bench is given a new look with a slipcover featuring a pleated skirt and welting trim. Two coordinating fabrics are used to create additional interest.

Slipcovers
FOR OTTOMANS & BENCHES

Ottomans and benches are easy to slipcover. You can add as much or as little detail as you want to the slipcover design. A slipcover can be as simple as tying the corners of a rectangle of fabric to the legs of an ottoman using decorative cording. Or a cover can be stitched as for the ruffled stool cov- ers on pages 107 to 111. The cover can have a ruffled or box-pleated skirt. And for added detail you can insert welting into the seams or embellish the corners with tie tabs or lacing inserted through grommets as shown on pages 50 and 51.

HOW TO SEW A *P*LEATED SLIPCOVER FOR A BENCH

1 ...... Pin fabric to top of bench, easing or pleating out fullness around any corners or curves. Mark fabric around drop line for skirt, marking any radiating foldlines of pleats. Fold any pleats on marked lines and cut ½" (1.3 cm) outside marked drop line. Determine the desired skirt length and cut fabric 2½" (6.5 cm) longer to allow for 1" (2.5 cm) double-fold hems and ½" (1.3 cm) seam allowance at upper edge; determine width of skirt piece, allowing enough fullness for pleats and seams.

2 ...... Seam skirt pieces together. Stitch 1" (2.5 cm) double-fold hems as on page 59, step 31. Pleat fabric. Make and apply welting to top bench piece as on page 43. Stitch skirt to top bench piece in ½" (1.3 cm) seam allowance. Cut ties as on page 108. Make and attach ties for securing slipcover to bench as on pages 110 and 111, steps 8 and 9.

Button-tufted CUSHIONS

Add seating comfort to wooden chairs and benches with simple knife-edge, button-tufted cushions. The lightly padded inner cushion is created by covering a piece of foam with a layer of polyester upholstery batting. The button tufting prevents the cushion from shifting inside the cover and also adds detailing. Place one button on the top and one on the bottom of the cushion, and pull them tight with strands of thread to create an indentation. Welting can be inserted into the seam for additional interest.

You may want to make the covered buttons and welting from a fabric that contrasts with that of the seat cushion. Checked and striped fabrics can create interesting effects when used for welting.

Secure the seat cushion to the chairs or benches with ties, if necessary. Place a set of ties near each back corner of the cushion for securing it to the back posts of the chair or bench.

LIST *of* MATERIALS

- ▶ Decorator fabric.
- ▶ Contrasting decorator fabric, for buttons and welting, optional.
- ▶ Polyurethane foam, 1" (2.5 cm) thick.
- ▶ Polyester upholstery batting; polyester fiberfill, optional.
- ▶ Cording, 5/32" (3.8 mm) in diameter, for welting, optional.
- ▶ Upholstery buttons or flat dressmaker buttons with strong shank; two for each button placement.
- ▶ Buttonhole twist or carpet thread; long needle with large eye.

CUTTING DIRECTIONS

Make the pattern and cut the fabric, foam, and batting following steps 1 to 3 on page 100. For the optional welting, cut 1 5/8" (4 cm) bias fabric strips; piece the strips as necessary to make a length that is equal to the circumference of the cushion plus at least 1" (2.5 cm) overlap at the ends. For each tie, cut two 1 1/2" (3.8 cm) fabric strips 10" to 16" (25.5 to 40.5 cm) long.

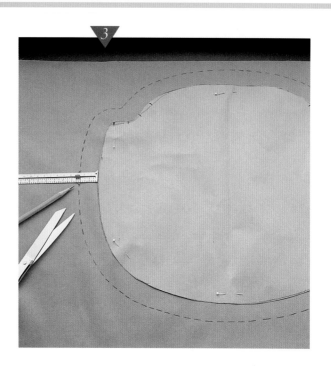

1...... Make a paper pattern of seat to be covered by cushion, as on page 104; simplify shape as necessary. Mark pattern for placement of ties, if desired.

2...... Cut two pieces of polyester upholstery batting, using pattern. Position pattern on foam; trace, using marking pen. Cut foam 1/4" (6 mm) inside marked line, using electric or serrated knife.

3...... Position the pattern on wrong side of decorator fabric. Mark cutting line 1" (2.5 cm) from edge of pattern; this allows 1/2" (1.3 cm) for the seam allowances and 1/2" (1.3 cm) for the thickness of the foam and batting. Cut the cushion top on marked line. Cut cushion bottom, using cushion top as pattern.

4...... Make welting, if desired, and apply to cushion top as on page 43. Make ties, if desired, as on page 83, step 4. Pin ties to the right side of seat top at markings, with raw edges even; stitch in place.

5...... Position cushion top and bottom with right sides together and raw edges even. Stitch 1/2" (1.3 cm) seam; leave center opening along back edge for inserting cushion. Trim the seam allowances and clip curves. If welting is not used, press seam open. Turn right side out; lightly press.

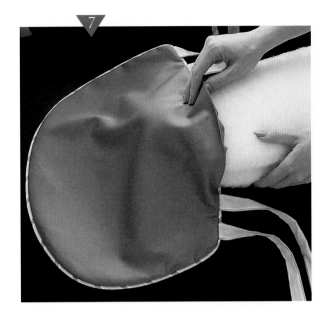

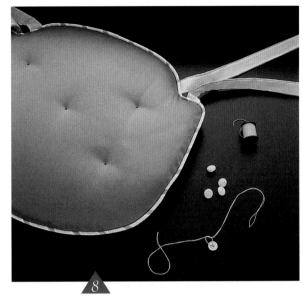

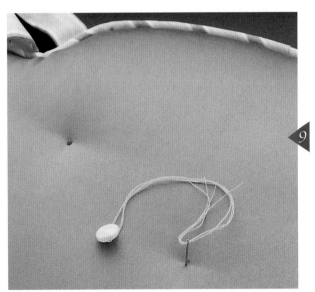

6..... Place foam between layers of batting; hand-baste edges of batting together, encasing foam as shown in photo on page 111, step 11.

7..... Fold foam in half; insert into fabric cover. Flatten foam, smoothing fabric over batting. Insert polyester fiberfill into corners, if necessary. Slipstitch opening closed.

8..... Pin-mark button placement on both sides of cushion as desired. Cut two or three 18" (45 cm) strands of buttonhole twist or carpet thread; insert all strands through button shank, and secure at middle of thread length with a double knot.

9..... Insert the ends of the thread strands through the eye of a long needle. Insert needle through cushion to back side. Remove strands from needle; divide strands into two groups.

10 .... Thread second button on one group of threads; tie a single knot, using both thread groups; pull until buttons are tight against cushion, creating indentation. Wrap the thread two or three times around the button shank. Tie a double knot; trim thread tails.

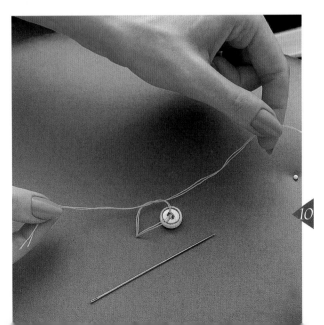

Chair & Bench PADS

Liven up wooden or resin patio chairs and benches with colorful pads. These lightly padded reversible seat cushions are simple to sew and feature bias binding around the edges.

Make your own bias binding for a customized look, using a bias tape maker as shown on page 106. Or, for quick construction, use purchased bias binding.

LIST *of* MATERIALS

► Decorator fabric.

► ½" (1.3 cm) high-density firm polyurethane foam.

► ½" (1.3 cm) single-fold bias tape; or fabric and ¾" (2 cm) bias tape maker.

► Glue stick.

Outdoor seat cushions add color and comfort to patio furniture. Left, a custom pad is made to fit a wooden bench.

Resin chair (below) is fitted with a colorful, shaped seat pad.

CHAIR OR BENCH PAD

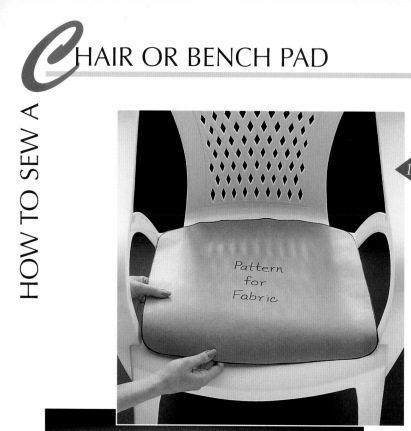

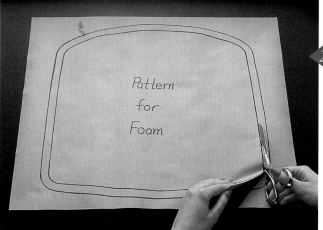

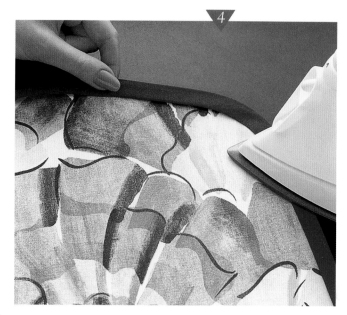

1...... Make a paper pattern of chair or bench seat to be covered by pad, rounding any sharp corners. Cut pattern; check fit. This pattern is used for cutting the fabric.

2...... Trace pattern on separate piece of paper; mark cutting line 5/8" (1.5 cm) in from traced line. Cut pattern on inner marked line. This pattern is used for cutting the foam.

3...... Cut the pad front and pad back from decorator fabric, using pattern for fabric. Place pattern for foam on the polyurethane foam; trace, using marking pen. Cut foam on marked line, using rotary cutter or scissors.

4...... Make bias tape (page 106), if desired; or use purchased bias tape. Press bias tape into curved shape to match shape of pad. To prevent puckering, stretch tape slightly as you press.

5 ..... Center foam on wrong side of pad back; place pad front over foam, right side up, matching raw edges of fabric. Pin layers together.

6 ..... Machine-baste ¼" (6 mm) seam around pad, using zipper foot.

7 ..... Apply small amount of glue stick to seam allowance of pad back. Finger-press wide side of bias tape into position, with raw edges of pad fabric at foldline of tape; overlap ends of tape about 1".

8 ..... Turn pad over. Glue-baste the narrow side of the tape to the seam allowance of pad front, using small amount of glue stick. Join ends of the tape by folding under ¼" (6 mm) on overlapping end; glue-baste.

9 ..... Stitch along inner edge of tape, using zipper foot, with narrow edge of tape facing up.

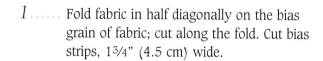

HOW TO MAKE

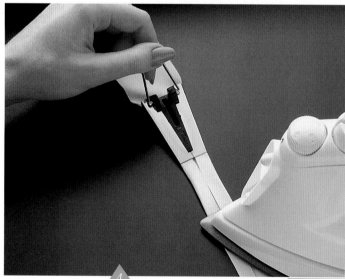

1 ...... Fold fabric in half diagonally on the bias grain of fabric; cut along the fold. Cut bias strips, 1¾" (4.5 cm) wide.

2 ...... Join strips, right sides together, by placing them at right angles, offset ¼" (6 mm); strips will form a "V." Stitch ¼" (6 mm) seam across the ends. Press seams open; trim seam allowances even with edges. Raw edges match on long edges after seams are stitched.

3 ...... Thread pointed end of the bias strip through channel at wide end of tape maker, bringing point out at narrow end. Using pin, pull fabric through slot opening; pin the point of strip to pressing surface.

4 ...... Press folded bias strip as you pull tape maker the length of the strip. Tape maker automatically folds raw edges to center of strip.

5 ...... Fold bias tape lengthwise, with folded edge on bottom extending a scant ⅛" (3 mm) beyond folded edge of upper layer; press.

Ruffled
STOOL COVERS

Wooden stools make convenient seating at a breakfast nook or counter, either for casual dining or for resting while you prepare food. Padded with foam, this ruffled stool cover adds comfort to a wooden stool.

Ruffled stool covers can be made for stools that are already padded, or the padding can be included in the stool cover. To add padding to the stool cover, use polyurethane foam.

The instructions that follow include a self-lined skirt, which adds body and eliminates the need for a hem. If a heavyweight fabric is used, the skirt may be cut shorter and narrow-hemmed instead.

RUFFLED STOOL COVER

LIST of MATERIALS

▶ Mediumweight fabric; 1½ yd. (1.4 m) is usually sufficient for one stool cover.

▶ Cording, for welting; 1½ yd. (1.4 m) is usually sufficient for one stool cover.

▶ Cord, such as pearl cotton, for gathering the ruffle.

▶ Polyurethane foam, 2" (5 cm) thick.

▶ Upholstery batting.

CUTTING DIRECTIONS

Make a pattern for cutting the foam by tracing around the top of the wooden stool. Mark a circle this size on the foam; cut the foam, using an electric knife or serrated knife.

For the cover top, cut one circle of fabric, 1" (2.5 cm) larger than the top of the stool, to allow for ½" (1.3 cm) seam allowance.

For the side of the stool cover, cut a boxing strip 1" (2.5 cm) wider than the thickness of the foam, with the length of the boxing strip 1" (2.5 cm) longer than the circumference around the top of the stool.

For a self-lined ruffled skirt with a finished length of 5" (12.5 cm), cut a rectangle of fabric on the crosswise or lengthwise grain, 11" (28 cm) wide by twice the circumference of the stool, piecing the strip, if necessary.

For the welting around the cover top, cut 1½" (3.8 cm) bias strips of fabric, with the combined length of the strips equal to the circumference of the stool top plus 3" (7.5 cm).

For the ties that secure the cover to the legs of the stool, cut eight 2½" x 12" (6.5 x 30.5 cm) fabric strips on the lengthwise or crosswise grain; two ties are used at each leg.

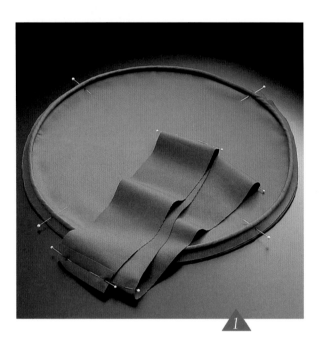

1...... Make welting and apply to cover top as on page 43. Stitch the short sides of boxing strip together, right sides together, in a ½" (1.3 cm) seam; press seam open. Fold the boxing strip into fourths; pin-mark upper and lower edges. Fold cover top into fourths; pin-mark.

2...... Pin upper edge of boxing strip to the cover top, matching pin marks; clip boxing strip within seam allowance as necessary, and ease boxing strip to fit.

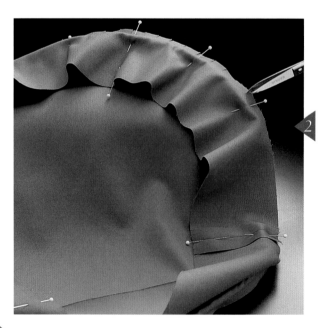

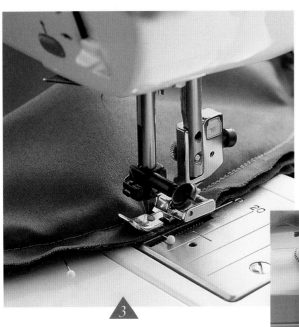

3

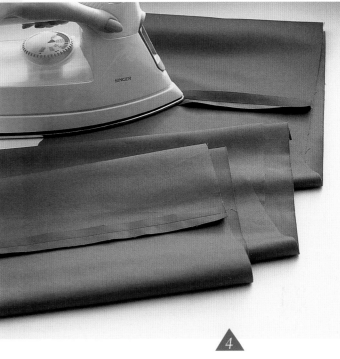

4

5

3 ...... Stitch boxing strip to the cover top in ½" (1.3 cm) seam, taking care to avoid stitching any tucks; stitch with cover top facing up.

4 ...... Stitch the skirt pieces together in ½" (1.3 cm) seams, right sides together; stitch ends together, forming continuous strip. Press seams open.

5 ...... Fold skirt in half lengthwise, wrong sides together; press.

continued

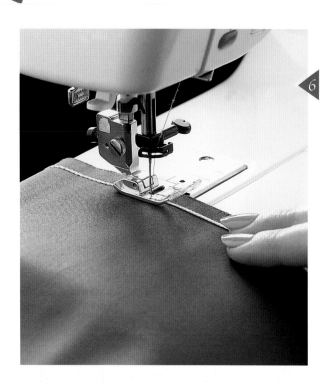

6 ..... Zigzag over a cord, a scant ½" (1.3 cm) from the raw edges of the skirt.

7 ..... Fold the skirt into fourths; pin-mark. Align upper edge of skirt to the lower edge of boxing strip, matching pin marks; gather to fit by pulling on the cord. Pin in place, matching raw edges; stitch ½" (1.3 cm) seam.

8 ..... Fold ½" (1.3 cm) to wrong side at one end of tie. Press the tie in half lengthwise, wrong sides together. Fold each edge to the center; press. Refold at center; press. Repeat for remaining ties.

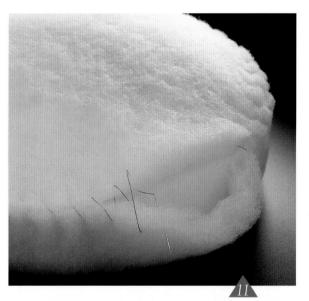

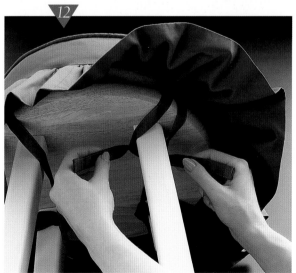

9 . . . . . Stitch along folded lengthwise edge of tie and across folded end.

10 . . . . Divide ruffle seam into fourths; pin-mark. Pin two ties to ruffle at each pin mark; align unfinished ends of ties to raw edge of ruffle. Stitch the ties in place along seamline. Finish seam at lower end of boxing strip, using zigzag or overlock stitch. Omit step 11 if purchased stool has padded seat.

11 . . . . Cover the foam with a layer of upholstery batting; hand-baste batting in place. Place foam into cover.

12 . . . . Place the cover on the stool with ties at legs of stool. Secure the ties around legs.

INDEX

Creative Publishing, Inc.

President: Iain Macfarlane
Executive V. P.: William B. Jones
Group Director, Book Development:
  Zoe Graul

Creative Textiles™
SLIPCOVERS
Created by: The Editors of Cowles
Creative Publishing, Inc.

Creative Director:
Lisa Rosenthal

Senior Managing Editor:
Elaine Perry

Project Manager: Amy Friebe

Art Director: Mark Jacobson

Editors: Dawn Anderson,
Linda Neubauer

Copy Editor: Janice Cauley

Desktop Publishing Specialist:
Laurie Kristensen

Project & Prop Stylists:
Coralie Sathre, Joanne Wawra

Lead Samplemaker: Carol Pilot

Samplemakers: Arlene Dohrman,
Virginia Mateen, Nancy Sundeen

Technical Photo Stylists:
Bridget Haugh, Nancy Sundeen

Studio Services Manager:
Marcia Chambers

Staff Photographers: Rex Irmen,
Gregory Wallace

Publishing Production Manager:
Kim Gerber

Printed on American paper by:
  Quebecor Printing
00 99 98 97 / 5 4 3 2 1

Cowles Creative Publishing, Inc. offers
a variety of how-to books. For information write:
  Cowles Creative Publishing
    Subscriber Books
  5900 Green Oak Drive
  Minnetonka, MN 55343